Hour of the Women

Pomerania in the Third Reich.

Enlarged detail (*below*) shows the area around Stolp in Eastern Pomerania with the 1938 border (and with Polish place-names after 1945).

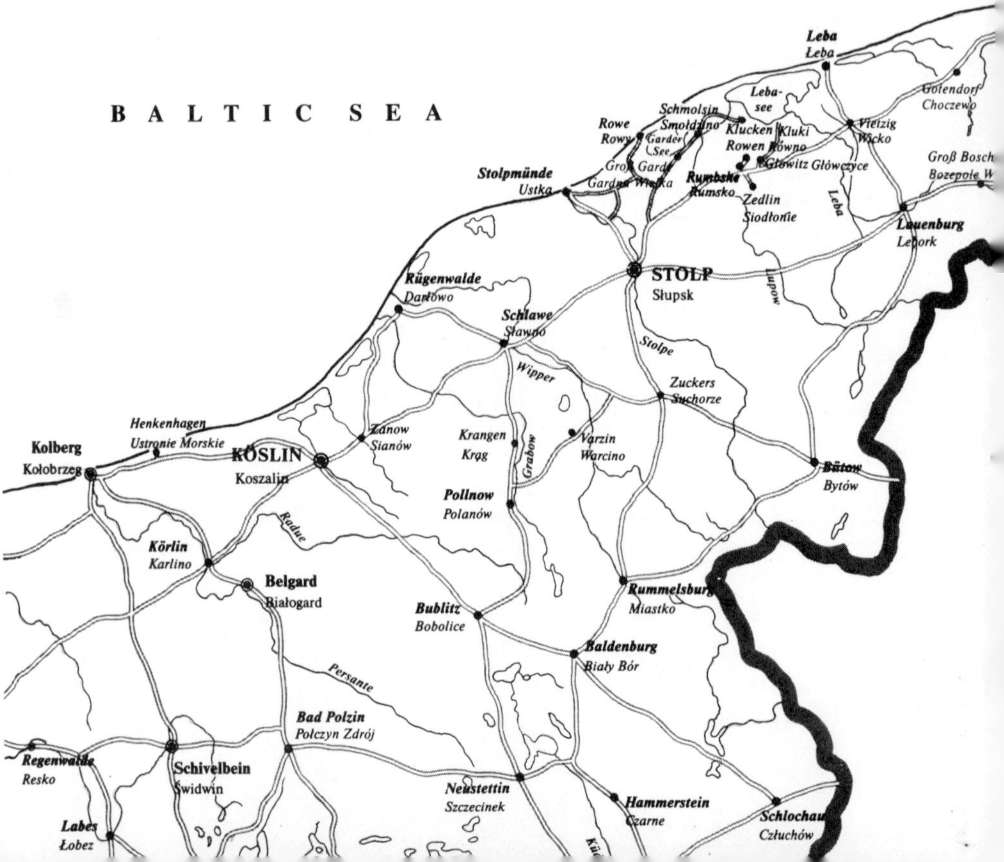

BALTIC SEA
Leba
Łeba
Leba-see
Schmolsin
Smołdzino
Rowe
Rowy
Garder See
Klucken
Kluki
Rowen
Równo
Glowitz
Główczyce
Groß Gard
Gardna Wielka
Rumbske
Rumsko
Zedlin
Siodłonie
Stolpmünde
Ustka
Gotendorf
Choczewo
Vietzig
Wicko
Groß Bosch
Bozepole W
Leba
Lauenburg
Lebork
STOLP
Słupsk
Lupow
Rügenwalde
Darłowo
Schlawe
Sławno
Stolpe
Wipper
Zuckers
Suchorze
Henkenhagen
Ustronie Morskie
Kolberg
Kołobrzeg
KÖSLIN
Koszalin
Zanow
Sianów
Krangen
Krąg
Grabow
Varzin
Warcino
Bütow
Bytów
Pollnow
Polanów
Radue
Körlin
Karlino
Belgard
Białogard
Rummelsburg
Miastko
Bublitz
Bobolice
Baldenburg
Biały Bór
Persante
Bad Polzin
Połczyn Zdrój
Regenwalde
Resko
Schivelbein
Świdwin
Neustettin
Szczecinek
Hammerstein
Czarne
Schlochau
Człuchów
Labes
Łobez

CHRISTIAN VON KROCKOW

Hour of the Women

Based on an oral narrative
by Libussa Fritz-Krockow

Translated from the German
by Krishna Winston

Edward Burlingame Books
An Imprint of HarperCollins*Publishers*

This book was first published in Germany in 1988 under the title *Die Stunde der Frauen*. Copyright © 1988 Deutsche Verlags-Anstalt GmbH, Stuttgart.

FIRST EDITION

Designed by Barbara DuPree Knowles
Frontispiece map by Frank Ronan

LIBRARY OF CONGRESS CATALOGING-IN-PUBLICATION DATA
Krockow, Christian, Graf von.
[Stunde der Frauen. English]
Hour of the women / Christian von Krockow; based on an oral narrative by Libussa Fritz-Krockow; translated from the German by Krishna Winston.—1st ed.
p. cm.
Translation of: Die Stunde der Frauen.
ISBN 0-06-016472-7
1. Fritz-Krockow, Libussa. 2. World War, 1939–1945—Refugees. 3. World War, 1939–1945—Pomerania (Germany and Poland) 4. World War, 1939–1945—Women—Pomerania (Germany and Poland) 5. Refugees, Political—Pomerania (Germany and Poland)—Biography. 6. Pomerania (Germany and Poland)—History. I. Fritz-Krockow, Libussa. II. Title.
D809.P64K7613 1991
940.53'15033104381—dc20 89-46562

91 92 93 94 95 CG/RRD 10 9 8 7 6 5 4 3 2 1

Contents

Preface

My sister, Libussa, first told me this story, bit by bit, on long winter evenings. It deals with the dark years in Germany between 1944 and 1947 and takes us east, across the Oder, to remote Pomerania.

Libussa's story is true and turns on terrible events. It shows the darker side of human nature, but also what strength there is in us to recover our humanity.

It also sheds a special light on German history. Our notions of right and wrong, our sense of order, our values have for centuries been formed one-sidedly: they are masculine to a fault, Protestant, Prussian, and soldierly. Self-sacrifice in the name of ideals. Obedience to the state and to superiors. Readiness to serve and fight even unto death. It is from these values that our achievements as well as our destruction have come. Our conditioning pushed us toward an either/or rigidity: friend or enemy, all or nothing, triumph or defeat.

But in defeat, when it suddenly materializes, these masculine principles lose their power and value. Survival in defeat, and, ultimately, in life itself, requires something else. This "something else" is at the heart of this book.

CHRISTIAN, COUNT KROCKOW

Hour of the Women

One Last Grand Celebration

Wedding's Eve

"Jobst-Werner Adam, Baron Oldershausen, Captain." The old-fashioned quill pen scratched along, got snagged on the paper, spattered a little ink. From the wall the Führer gazed down approvingly, hand on hip; after all, he needed soldiers. Under "Children," the family record book already given to the engaged couple had room for ten entries, or was it twelve? In any case, more than enough. The bottom of the page carried the printed admonition:

> Marriage is not an end in itself; it must serve the greater end of preserving and increasing the race and the species. Therein alone lies its significance and its high purpose.
>
> —ADOLF HITLER

But how unseemly: right next to the Führer, something kept dripping into a sink. Herr Jürgens, town clerk of Glowitz, in the county of Stolp in Pomerania, also served as our photographer, present at baptisms, confirmations, and weddings in all the villages around. He had just hung up a batch of prints to dry.

Now came my turn: "Eva-Margarete Libussa, Baroness Oldershausen . . ." But I had run out of space on the form.

People in these parts usually had names that were short and sweet: Karl Peske, Emil Klick, Grete Musch. For a moment Herr Jürgens seemed at a loss. But I could not truncate my name, so he pointed to the space for the next entry, and I dipped the pen again: "née von der Wickerau, Countess Krockow."

Now the witnesses had to sign. First came the "old Glowitzer," born in 1859, brother of my grandmother, the "Iron Countess," who had just died the year before. With his usual grumbling, he had succeeded in confusing poor Herr Jürgens, who was trying to pronounce the official blessing. Great-Uncle Gerhard signed himself "Gerhard Eugen Friedrich Lorenz Karl von Puttkamer." Next came Father Jesko, as we all called him, actually my stepfather, whom my mother had married after the death of my father: "Jesko Ludwig Günther Nikolaus, Baron Puttkamer." These barons were in some ways the outsiders among the many-headed Pomeranian Puttkamer clan, for it was not they who owned the large estates. But barons or not, they were all called Jesko or Jesco, or occasionally, in a wild flight of fancy, Hans- or Karl-Jesco. And that made Great-Uncle Gerhard something of an outsider here.

He was muttering to himself again now, louder than before, for in the meantime Herr Jürgens was presenting the official gift: the Führer's *Mein Kampf.* "For the newly wedded couple, with best wishes for a happy and fruitful union, from the city government," was stamped on the flyleaf. Underneath was the date, written in by hand: Friday, June 16, 1944. Hat on, cane in hand, and the old Glowitzer was off. Without saying goodbye.

"That old fox! That rascal! After him!" Father Jesko exclaimed. For the hat left on the hook was not Jesko's exquisitely elegant summer boater but a piece of headgear battered almost beyond recognition, its original green long since discolored into a grubby gray-brown. Great-Uncle Gerhard must have worn that hat for a good half century, rain or shine, out in the fields, in the stables, or for going to church. "You have to look sharp," he said craftily when we finally caught up with him.

Back to the carriage, waiting for us outside the registry office. The coachman, Karl Pallas, used his whip only as a badge of office; a soft click of the tongue and a flick of the reins, and Swallow and Sunset moved off at a trot. They were snorting in their eagerness to get back to their stall. Their hooves beat a rhythm on the road from Neu-Klenzin to Rumbske. What a magnificent day! In the barely perceptible breeze, a few puffy clouds sailed beneath the sun. To our right, on the slope of the aptly named Wedding Hill, the wheat was ripening. Larks trilled. From the left wafted the scent of new-mown hay on the broad meadows. Storks stalked along with great dignity. A heron stood motionless by the ditch. Just a bit farther off, we spied deer, among them already a few fawns; they were sitting down and chewing their cud, undisturbed by the passing carriage. Images of peace.

From day to day the fighting in Normandy is intensifying. During the first days after the invasion, the enemy focused his efforts on establishing a foothold along the coast. Now he is attempting to extend his bridgehead on all sides. With volleys of heavy naval gunfire, constant aerial attacks, and advances by freshly deployed infantry and armored units on both sides, the fighting is approaching a climax.[1]

Polterabend—the eve of the wedding. Some of the guests had already arrived, relatives of Jobst's from Hanover and Holstein, girlfriends of mine from Berlin. After dinner we had a fire lit in the fireplace, more for coziness than for warmth. Fräulein Rahn, the housekeeper, known affectionately as Rahnini, recited rhymes of her own invention in Silesian dialect; they of course contained allusions to Pomeranian originals, such as the verses recited at harvest festivals before the war:

We wish our gracious lady a rose garden
Where she can await her darlin'.

Or, from another year:

We wish Countess Libussa a bower of jasmine
Where she may await him.

Now we had a new verse:

White dress amidst leaves of green,
It really was high time, you see.

Ah, Rahnini, if you only knew. I was indeed awaiting a "him" four years ago; our betrothal long since agreed upon. But then a terse message reported that my fiancé had "failed to return from a mission over enemy territory."

Outside, the poltergeists were busy, smashing quantities of crockery on the stairs leading up to the manor, as though we had as much to spare as ever. Custom dictated that the newlyweds should sweep up the shards the following morning, with the husband wielding the broom and the bride the dustpan. If the roles became reversed, that would be a terrible omen: contrary to the established order in the world, the wife would rule the roost and the man would be henpecked.

We drank plentifully and well. At one point Jobst picked up his guitar and sang, more loudly than melodiously. He sang of Marushka, "the most beautiful girl in Poland, or in all the world." And "My papa was a Cossack / In the Urals is my home . . ." What if the Führer had heard that!

I had known Jobst for seven years, since 1937, when he and my brother became friends as cadets. They were inseparable. I always called him my big brother. His friend fell near Warsaw in September 1939, and my other brother soon followed. Gone, never to return, first one, then the other. Jobst survived, though now with a long, deep scar from a head wound. He wooed me persistently, and for a long time I turned him down: one cannot marry one's brother. Or was I trying to reject fate, which dictated another course to me than the one my heart had originally chosen? Be that as it might, Rahnini was probably right in saying it was "high time." The list of our dead was growing ever longer.

Prussian Precision

With the war in its fifth year, one might have thought grim austerity would be the watchword—a small, quiet wedding with just family and a few friends. Was it permissible to celebrate as though it were peacetime? Was it even possible?

"But of course—now more than ever!" Father Jesko had exclaimed, brushing aside my doubts. "It should be the way it's always been. Just leave everything to me. And who knows . . ." A slight hesitation, a moment's gloom. "Never mind! One last grand celebration—we'll show them, all of them." He did not specify who "all of them" were: envious folk, the enemy, fanatics in brown shirts, friends and neighbors, we ourselves?

"Leave everything to me": among his talents, Father had a gift and a passion for planning, directing, and organizing on a grand scale. As a cadet, as a page at court, as the Prussian officer he had once been and still was, he had mastered the precision essential for general-staff operations. His own precision resulted, quite unintentionally and in all good faith, in a kind of bossiness. He thought that all the others tended to be too vague about things, creating havoc with their casualness and sloppiness, so it fell to him to order them around and keep them under control—for their own good, of course.

Actually the planning had begun a long time before. From the French campaign of 1940 Father Jesko had returned with a crate of the finest champagne, which he stored in the cellar, giving strict orders that it was not to be touched. "Libussa's wedding wine" had been there even longer: it was my real father who had bought it, thinking far ahead. Paris had also provided the red silk for the dress I wore for the wedding's eve; also for the lining of the white wool cloak woven by my mother. When Father discovered that Jobst's orderly came from a lacemaking family in the Erz Mountains, he loaded the young man down with Pomeranian sausages and hams and had him sent home on special leave to bring back lovely lace of peacetime quality for my wedding dress and veil.

And so it went, item after item. Emil Klick, the steward in Rowen, one of the villages belonging to the estate, had relatives in Klucken, a fishing village on the other side of the moor, by Lake Leba. They provided us with magnificent pike. Drambusch the forester shot three deer, and we had larded venison roast, a real delicacy, to complement the roast veal. For days before the great event, Marie the cook was receiving a constant stream of visitors. The tenant farmers' wives and the estate hands brought whatever they had, especially butter. Oodles of butter; some of it went to the baker in Glowitz, for the wedding cake.

Mother wanted to decorate the table in red and white rhododendrons. But of course we could not strip the bushes in front of the manor. So she rang up neighbors in Grossendorf, Zemmin, Selesen, and whole laundry baskets full of blossoms arrived early in the morning, brought by liveried servants who would assist our own maid Frieda and old Vietzke. Meanwhile village women spent days sitting in a barn weaving garlands.

And then there was the general-staff plan, all worked out on paper, with carbon copies sent to all parties concerned, accompanied by notes threatening stern reprisals for even a few seconds' delay:

0825 HOURS Pallas and Peske arrive station with carriages
0829 HOURS Train arrives
0906 HOURS Frieda: breakfast for guests
1010 HOURS All coachmen: carriages
1020 HOURS Depart for church
1050 HOURS Arrive at church
1100 HOURS Service begins
1135 HOURS Service concludes and carriages
1145 HOURS Depart from church

The schedule continued in the same vein through the following morning: "0500: Breakfast; 0550: Carriages; 0600: Depart for station; 0616: Train departs." Even Herr Sprondel, the superintendent from Stargard, invited specially because he had confirmed me years before, when he was our local pastor, received a carbon copy, to make sure he kept his sermon short.

In spite of all the planning, mishaps occurred. The garlands decorating the house were supposed to sport ribbons in both families' colors. We Krockows had black and gold, the Oldershausens red and gold. When Father went out to inspect, he almost had a stroke: black-red-gold, the colors of the Weimar Republic, which he, Prussian, monarchist, patriotic nationalist, and officer in the Stahlhelm, had always loathed. Quickly the visiting Oldershausens were sacrificed, leaving only the bridal colors on display.

But the war took a more serious toll on the festivities. Ten days earlier, the Allies had begun their invasion of the continent by landing in Normandy, and since then all military leaves had been canceled. One after the other the regrets poured in; not even my younger brother could come, though he had just turned seventeen and was not a regular soldier, only an assistant at the antiaircraft installation in Swinemünde. The much-discussed and prettily painted seating chart landed in the wastepaper basket, and the grand celebration seemed in danger of degenerating into a tiresome ladies' circle. Dignified graybeards like the "old Glowitzer" could hardly be expected to dance the night away, nor would the young ladies find them particularly entertaining.

But Father Jesko thought of a way out. A training unit of the Lüneburg Horse had recently been stationed in Stolp. Apparently we owed this fortunate arrangement to Field Marshal von Mackensen, honorary commander of the Stolp Regiment. To his dismay, this regiment had been ordered to exchange its horses for bicycles. At that, the old hussar, who wanted mounted men under his command, managed to get the Lüneburg unit transferred to East Pomerania.

Father rang up the commander and asked whether he might help us out with some officers. The band from the other unit, the one on bicycles, was coming in any case.

The commander saw no obstacle; the twenty-four-hour "wedding detail" could be classified as special duty—it had nothing whatsoever to do with leave. The requisite number of men arrived punctually on the 8:29 train. Unexpectedly, the group even included an Oldershausen, a cousin of Jobst's.

The Fortune of Edenhall

Another perfect summer day. Not a cloud in the sky, and just a light sea breeze to keep the heat at bay.

The carriages drew up punctually at ten o'clock, prettily garlanded. First came the two carriages for the bridal couple and the bride's parents, then two open farm wagons for the guests. The wagons had been fitted, as for the hunt in winter, with planks along the sides as seats and with a step at the back.

Everything was so perfect, it annoyed me to see Jobst putting on his helmet. "Must you wear that thing? Think of your wound; you'll end up with a headache again."

"It's not that 'thing'; it's my steel helmet. Besides, I'm wearing it because that's what the regulations call for."

"Good heavens! Regulations. So why are the other officers just wearing their peaked caps?"

"They're not getting married, are they?"

"Well, I promise I won't hit you with the rolling pin until later, not at the altar."

Father Jesko, who had joined us, wearing his major's uniform and his cap, was not amused. "That's enough, Libussa. Ten-eighteen! Helmet on, and all aboard!"

Glowitz was thronged. Hundreds of people had come from the surrounding villages, even some curiosity-seekers from as far away as Stolp, where the newspaper had carried an announcement of the event. At most, half of the crowd could fit into the church. Even the children had successfully pleaded to be let out of school, as we had done when I was a child, writing on the blackboard:

The sky is blue, the weather's fair,
Oh, teacher, please, let's go to the fair!

The teachers had probably been only too glad to give in. The head teacher from the school serving Rumbske and Rowen had been practicing a hymn with his charges, which they now sang. It was as though all those present, great and small, young and old, wanted to engrave in their memories this last grand celebration.

Among the traditional duties of the bride was "throwing buns." The baker had been supplied with butter and sugar for the express purpose of making them, and while the ceremony was taking place, he loaded into the carriage a laundry basket full to the brim with those sweet round buns elsewhere called "snails." As we drove off, I tossed them to the children.

But the horses wanted to trot, and soon we had left the crowd behind, before I could empty my basket. Just a little later, as we pulled into Rumbske, the remaining buns became the cause of the first argument in my married life. Outside their quarters, the French POWs had lined up along the road to the manor and were waving and shouting, *"Vivent les mariés!"* I waved back and threw them buns.

I felt a kick in my shins, and Jobst hissed at me, "Stop that! It's strictly forbidden! Remember, they're prisoners of war!"

What nonsense; we thought of them as "our" Frenchmen. At Christmas they got their roast rabbit, at Easter their painted eggs, as was only proper. They had been with us for four years by now, had learned to understand the Pomeranian Low German dialect, and had taken over all the responsible jobs from which our German men had been dragged away by the war. They looked after the horses and raised the foals; they drove the tractors and the old steam plow. What would have become of the greenhouse and the gardens without "Garden Pierre"? And imperceptibly, behind their own backs, so to speak, these exiles had come to take pride in their accomplishments, to identify with their duties. Just a little while ago, Vietzke, loyal servant to the family for decades, who had been put in charge of the granary, had reported in alarm, "Baron, the oats keeps disappearing." An investigation revealed that the culprits were the French workers, who were housed on the lower floor of the granary. They were not stealing for themselves, however, but for "their" horses' nose bags.

Impulsively I seized the basket and tossed the whole thing, with all the remaining buns, to the POWs. Jobst stared grimly straight ahead. As we rolled through the gates and down the avenue of ancient lindens toward the manor, a gentle breeze unfurled the flag bearing the Krockow arms high above the roof.

A grand celebration: in the tradition of Pomeranian weddings, the guests' well-being was more than lavishly provided for, and all were repeatedly urged to partake. A substantial coffee spread followed on the heels of champagne and canapés. A buffet supper interrupted the dancing at midnight, and a hearty breakfast concluded the night's festivities.

But the heart of the celebration was the splendid banquet, lasting three hours, from hors d'oeuvres and soup to dessert and coffee. Birch branches decorated the hall. Against the heavy damask tablecloths, the rhododendron blossoms glowed in the light of a hundred candles. Laughter and a babble of voices filled the air as Vietzke, in his capacity as majordomo, discreetly directed the entrances and exits of his little troupe of platter- and bowl-carriers.

Great-Uncle Gerhard, who, as the oldest guest, occupied a place of honor across from the bridal couple, tapped his glass. He gazed critically around him and in a very loud voice declaimed, "As our ancestors did before us, let us rise and drink the first toast to our commander in chief." A pause while we stood up, with much scraping of chairs; then silence. And then, louder still, "Long live His Majesty, the King of Prussia!" A quick glance around at the bewildered officers, who did not know the old Glowitzer, and whom he did not know, either, and then, as a half-audible afterthought, "And Herr Hitler too."

The surprise and consternation had barely given way to a fresh babble of voices, with laughter and giggling here and there, when Father Jesko pushed back his chair.

He stepped out of the room for a moment, and when he came back, a quiver of apprehension ran through me. He was cradling a goblet in both hands, and he gently set it down on the table. "The Fortune of Edenhall," or at least that was the name this venerable heirloom had borne in our family ever since Uhland's ballad was published:

From Edenhall the youthful lord
Lets festive trumpet blasts ring out.
He rises at the groaning board
And then amidst the drunken mirth,
"Bring the fortune of Edenhall!" is his shout.

Our ancestor Reinhold von Krockow had brought the goblet back from France in the sixteenth century. It was a present to him from the prince of Navarre, later to become famous as good King Henry IV. This ancestor had served many masters as a diplomat. In addition, or perhaps in particular, he had helped finance wars throughout Europe, supporting the king of Poland in a "campayne against the Muscovites," as the chronicle had it, and later aided the French Huguenots, led by Prince Henry. But the Huguenots were butchered in the Saint Bartholomew's Day Massacre in 1572, and Henry converted to Catholicism to gain the crown of France (*"Paris vaut bien une messe,"* he was said to have declared), and Reinhold never recovered the bulk of the 315,000 florins he had invested in the war. All he had to show for his efforts was the goblet, an emblem of the fragility of good fortune.

Now Father beckoned to Vietzke. I had never seen the goblet close up; it had hunting scenes carved into its crystal sides, and a golden knob graced the ornamental lid. Normally the treasure remained in its place of honor in the library, in a specially made glass case, with gilded molding and a gold lock. Custom dictated that the goblet be used only once in each generation: at the wedding of the family heir. The goblet had last been used during the First World War, for the wedding of my father and my mother. Father Jesko had Vietzke fill it with something even finer than champagne: my "wedding wine," a burgundy from the year of my birth. Father reminded everyone of the tradition, and said, "Libussa, your brothers Klaus-Wilhelm and Hans-Kaspar can no longer receive their legacy. They died for the Fatherland. But you shall have part of their inheritance. And you, Jobst, will now share in it. May the two of you never forget it; keep it safe! And now: drink, dear children!"

Truly a grand celebration, as though in defiance of time, which no one could really hold back. One long night, all too short, for dancing, and already dawn was breaking. No amount of heady exuberance could thwart Prussian precision:

0500 HOURS Breakfast
0550 HOURS Carriages
0600 HOURS Depart for station
0616 HOURS Train departs

The Bolted Gate

Autumn Homecoming

Along the Leopold Canal, northeast of Bruges, several Canadian attacks have been repulsed. Owing to casualties and the loss of over 300 tanks and armored personnel carriers, crippled by our forces between September 29 and October 6, the enemy's attacks along the Dutch-Belgian border have diminished in intensity. The enemy continues to exert pressure on the area north of Antwerp. Enemy tank spearheads, intended to break through north of Baarle-Nassau, have been beaten back, with many tanks destroyed.

Our own assaults on the enemy bridgehead southeast of Wageningen have gained ground; British counterattacks have failed. In the bulge south of Geilenkirchen, the enemy has attacked with renewed ferocity. In spite of our determined resistance, the enemy has achieved limited local breakthroughs, losing in the process 69 tanks, however.

Last night, waves of our fighter planes battered enemy troop emplacements in the Aachen area. The garrison of Fort Driant on the Moselle has repulsed powerful enemy onslaughts. Additional sections of the Parroy Forest have been cleared of enemy troops. To either side of Remiremont, the Americans have been reinforced by Moroccan and Algerian units. Fierce fighting continues, especially at the mouths of the valleys east of Remiremont.

From our fortifications and bases along the Atlantic come reports of artillery battles and successful raids by our shock troops.

Yesterday London again came under fire from V-1's.

In central Italy, bad weather has brought about a lull in the fighting. Localized enemy attacks on our positions on high ground to either side of the Florence-Bologna highway were stopped in their tracks by concerted firepower.

In the Balkans, the fighting against the partisans continues. Soviet tank spearheads reached the mouth of the Theiss River but were turned back in the region east of Belgrade. Here and in the vicinity of Zaječar, our grenadiers and Alpine troops are fighting fiercely against the advancing enemy troops. In the Hungarian marches, large concentrations of enemy troops launched a major attack from north of Arad, and after heavy fighting, advance troops reached the Kreisch Rapids. Our fighter planes mounted effective attacks on their columns. Further countermeasures have now been initiated. To the northwest of Thorenburg and along the Maros, numerous Bolshevik attacks have failed. Renewed fighting has begun in the wooded passes of the Carpathians.

On the lower Narew, the enemy's bridgehead north of Serock has been further narrowed by our attacks. South of Różan, the enemy suffered heavy casualties and is thus mounting only isolated and ineffectual attacks. Between the Memel and the upper Windau, a fierce defensive battle broke out. Our divisions offered stout resistance to a large enemy force advancing under air cover and succeeded in destroying numerous tanks.

American terror bombers with fighter cover have been mounting terror attacks on the capital, on Hamburg, Stralsund, and Stettin, while British squadrons have bombed the Rhineland and Westphalia, destroying residential areas of Dortmund and Bremen in night attacks. Last night a weaker formation of British planes again attacked Berlin. Fierce dogfights and antiaircraft guns brought down 72 aircraft over the Reich and the western battle zone, among them 54 four-engine bombers.[2]

From high summer to autumn was only a couple of months. But that period saw a transformation in the military map. The Americans were no longer fighting for the Atlantic fortifications but fighting for Aachen, and the Russians were no longer far away on the Dnieper but on the Vistula, on the edge of East Prussia.

In every letter, my mother wrote, "Do come home, child," with greater urgency each time. Since she had found out that I was pregnant, her words acquired more force, because she could appeal to my sense of duty: "It is not good to spend every night cowering in air-raid shelters; you must not think only of yourself now."

We were living in Krampnitz, near the northern boundary of Potsdam, close to Berlin. Jobst was assigned to a training unit. His wound was giving him trouble again, and he was also suffering from attacks of asthma, which made him, thank heavens, unfit for active duty at the front. By now the sirens wailed not only at night but more and more frequently in the daytime as well; the air vibrated with airplane engines, flak, and exploding bombs.

But perhaps another factor also came into play: between Jobst and me there was more and more tension. Before we married, I had thought I knew him very well, but I had not realized to what extent and how obsessively this man was a soldier. We could not walk down the street without his causing scenes that I found most embarrassing. He always wore his uniform, and the streets were thronged with soldiers; the regulations stipulated that every officer had to be saluted. If one of the soldiers failed to salute, or did not salute smartly enough to satisfy him, Captain von Oldershausen would fly into a rage and shout at the fellow at the top of his lungs. A few passersby would stop, and all of them would stare, while I dropped back or strolled on ahead, trying to look as though none of this had anything to do with me. But I could not overcome the embarrassment. To make it worse, the salute in question was the "Heil Hitler!"—compulsory for the army since the July 20 attempt on the Führer's life.

When I protested to Jobst, he reprimanded me sternly. Grand words rained down on my head: "troop morale," "military preparedness."

"But what in the world has that got to do with saluting smartly?"

"A great deal! Obedience, order, discipline: one mustn't let anything slip by, because once they're gone, you might as well give up."

Well, that resulted in a real shlamassel, and all because I had no appreciation for discipline.

After another bombing raid on Berlin, a particularly heavy one, Jobst, too, was convinced that I should leave. I packed my bags.

Actually it was amazing how well the city still functioned. The elevated municipal railway from Potsdam to the Stettin Station was still running, gliding along through a landscape of ruins. According to the timetable, the train to Pomerania left at 8:05, and sure enough, fifteen minutes before departure they were coupling it together. Just at that moment the sirens went off. Loudspeakers croaked: *"Achtung! Achtung!* Clear the platforms! Remain calm! Proceed to the designated shelters! *Achtung! Achtung!"* People did not proceed; they scurried along, falling, picking themselves up, running. A further announcement, while I stood there hesitating, loaded down with my luggage: "*Achtung! Achtung!* The train will depart immediately." I flung my suitcases into a carriage and scrambled in after them. Anything to get out of there!

Already the wheels were turning—"for victory," as posters everywhere proclaimed. The train picked up speed, accelerated, raced along, hurtling over switches, careening around bends. Peacetime speed limits no longer meant anything; this train was running for its life.

But not fast enough: to the steel hawks high in the sky it was just a sluggish worm, far easier to spot out in the open than amid the confusion of tracks and ruins in the city. Ten minutes, at most a quarter of an hour, had passed since departure when there was a sudden splintering crash: fighter-bombers! We were under attack. I threw myself down on the floor, under the seat, as if it offered any protection. A squealing of brakes, and the train shuddered to a halt.

I struggled to my feet, looked out the window. I saw a house, but it seemed to be moving, as in a surrealist film. The house tilted sideways in slow motion, stopped, tilted in the other direction, seemed to bow, lower and lower still. Then a cloud of dust.

Anything to get out of there! Crushed stone, the embankment, underbrush, trees, the safety of a copse. The firebirds were already wheeling back for more prey.

When the danger seemed past, the conductor's shout summoned the thirty or so passengers again. Broken glass everywhere, one carriage with a large opening gaping in its side, another riddled with holes. But because there were so few of us on the train, we were all unhurt, except for scrapes and bruises, ripped clothing. The wheels could still turn. "All aboard!" We continued on our way, very slowly and cautiously now, as far as Eberswalde. There the two damaged cars were uncoupled, and the train promptly set out again, as though nothing had happened. We reached Stettin barely an hour behind schedule.

The railway bridge over the Oder, gateway to East Pomerania. Relief, a sense of being home safe and sound. The familiar stations: Stargard, Ruhnow, Labes, known half affectionately, half mockingly as Scuff-Labes, because this was where "scuffs" were made, the wooden clogs worn summer and winter by young and old. Then Schivelbein, Belgard, Köslin, Schlawe. Soon I would be at my destination.

But another shock awaited me, a far more sinister image than houses toppling over beneath low-flying aircraft: somewhere between Schlawe and Stolp we passed masses of people, mostly women, armed with spades and shovels. For miles and miles, as far as the eye could see, they were digging a deep trench.

"What on earth are they doing?" I asked a soldier who had got on in Köslin.

"That's a tank trap, to stop Ivan."

"To stop him? But how?"

"Very simple: the tanks just roll along and straight into the trench. They fall on their backs like June bugs. That's the idea anyway."

"Will it work?"

"Well, it might, so long as Ivan doesn't have any grenades or any engineers with dynamite to make the sides cave in."

"But so much effort . . . Does that mean that if we live farther east they've already given us up?"

No reply. A long look, a hint of a shrug, silence.

Of Citadels and Treasure Chests

Things seemed almost the same as ever. Autumn in Pomerania always brought the potato harvest, with the estate lands in Rumbske, Rowen, and Zedlin alone accounting for almost a thousand acres. Everyone had to pitch in. I trudged across the field next to the heavy cart drawn by four horses. Up a ladder mounted on its side, a couple of strong Frenchmen shoved the *Rummeln,* wooden crates weighing a good 150 pounds when full. From a canister worn on a strap I handed them a stamp for each crate; these stamps would later be pasted into books and exchanged for cash at the estate office. During breaks in the work, we made bonfires of the potato vines; their fragrance hovered over the countryside.

In the next field over, Max and Moritz puffed away amid the stubble; these were the powerful steam-plow twins. They were stationed on opposite sides of the field, and the multi-shared plow moved back and forth between them on a steel cable. Their puffing had a triumphant sound to it; the small fry, the tractor, which had been trying to supplant these venerable dinosaurs, had been brought to a halt by a shortage of petroleum, while coal could still be had for the locomobiles, though it had to be supplemented with oak logs. The distillery ran on the same fuel and was still turning out spirits, potato flakes, and swill for the livestock. Yes, the work had not changed, even if German women and children were now working alongside French and Ukrainian POWs in Rumbske, Russians in Zedlin, and Americans in Rowen.

In this fall of 1944, East Pomerania seemed almost like a citadel of peace. Wailing sirens and panic were things people knew of only secondhand. Two streams of people, actually only trickles at this stage, converged here and found refuge. From the easternmost reaches of East Prussia, the Memel area, arrived a long column of wagons, drawn by curiously small, shaggy, but tough horses and carrying people with strange-sounding names. Lodgings were found for these people in the various villages, and the old term "trek" came back into use. From the opposite direction came fugitives from the bombing in the west, the Ruhr district; they, too, had unfamiliar names, which the village schoolchildren made fun of.

In the manor we sighed a bit and shoved closer together to make room, but in fact we were still a long way from being crowded. Our summer guests had turned into permanent residents: Uncle Biedermann and Aunt Deten, an elderly painter and his wife from Berlin, and Fräulein Trautmann from Wuppertal, a mildly eccentric spinster psychotherapist whom Mother had picked up somewhere. Not only people found refuge with us; the unflaggingly dignified Herr Grothe—to label him a servant would have grievously offended him—brought a large crate from Sommerswalde Castle near Berlin. It contained paintings of incalculable value—old Dutch masters, carefully removed from their frames and wrapped.

A bit later, a different sort of crate caused quite a stir. The manor house in Klenzin, which had stood empty for ten years, was now slated to become a home for evacuated children. First workmen moved in, and one of them came to Father Jesko, saying agitatedly, "Baron, I was checking the cellar walls, and one section sounded completely hollow. Probably a door, walled up. So I took a pry bar to the wall, just a bit, a couple of bricks. But behind it there's another cellar and maybe another beyond that. And there in the corner are a couple of crates, half in water, half covered with dust. Almost like coffins—no, more like chests, really . . ."

"So I was right!" Aunt Deten, gifted or cursed with a feel for the supernatural, was beside herself. "That's what I've been telling you all along! But you just laughed at me!"

True enough: back in 1930, when we lived at Klenzin for a few years after my father's death, Aunt Deten had a dream of a "lady in white." The ghost pointed to the ground in the corner of the room—approximately where those chests had now been discovered in the cellar. Aunt Deten had insisted that a treasure had to be down there. Of course my brothers and I wanted to rip up the floor immediately and start digging, and of course we were not allowed to. Yet that "lady in white" had merely indicated where to look; there had always been talk of buried treasure: the story had been handed down for over three hundred years from one generation of villagers and estate hands to the next. Or perhaps the tale grew out of a more practical consideration, disbelief that such a large house should have only a relatively small cellar under it.

It was an eerie story. The manor went back to the early seventeenth century, built just when the Thirty Years' War was beginning. How far off the war had seemed at first, in distant Bohemia. But inexorably, little by little, it had edged closer to Pomerania. And then, all of a sudden, it was there. Perhaps the landowners had hidden their valuables in the walled-up part of the cellar and had been forced to flee, then caught and killed by marauding Swedish soldiers before they could tell anyone where they had deposited their earthly goods.

The horrors of war were not documented solely in dusty old tales; concrete evidence existed, if you knew where to look. Out in the forest you could still see the remains of the "Swedish fortifications," as they were tellingly called. There was one set of them in the Wossek Woods near Rumbske, a second beyond Rowen along the road to the Leba Moor, and a third between Klenzin and Zedlin: deep hollows dug into hillsides, with earth berms thrown up around them. History did not record whether these fortifications provided safety or brought down destruction on the inhabitants. After all, doesn't greed for booty sharpen people's wits? Did the Swedish invaders set bloodhounds on the hastily erased trails, or did a cow low at the wrong moment? What good could axes and scythes do against assailants in armor? Questions without answers. One image of fear remained to us, compressed into a child's verse:

Pray, little one, pray!
The Swede is on his way!
The general's name is Oxenstern,
From him the children prayers will learn.

That verse could not be found in any schoolbook, but it was rooted deep in the folk memory, preserved and handed down to children and grandchildren.

Father Jesko had the hunting wagon hitched up. I went along; after all, Klenzin was part of my inheritance. Sure enough—through the hole in the cellar wall, by the beam of a flashlight, we glimpsed an extensive underground vault and, rising out of the water, two trunks that did indeed look like treasure chests.

My curiosity kindled, I asked, "Shouldn't we have them brought out right away?"

"No," Father Jesko replied, "leave them be. One mustn't destroy every mystery. And now is hardly the time for bringing out buried treasure."

"But when will it be the right time? In the summer, when the water level goes down?"

"Perhaps. We'll see."

"But—"

"But what?" Suddenly Father's voice had an edge to it: "Have you given any thought to where we should hide our silver in Rumbske?"

While the workmen carefully filled in the hole and plastered it over, we drove home in silence.

The Proper Way

In the manor in Rumbske, the kitchen was located belowground. From there a steep staircase led down to a long, almost forgotten passageway. It was dark and musty, with only a trace of light from a room off to one side, once used for slaughtering animals. At the end of the passage was the half-dilapidated "Octagon," at one time a taproom but long out of use. Legend had it that the local nobles forgathered there when they wished to be undisturbed. If the sun refused to shine for the harvest, they would come here to "drink the rain away"—keeping wet inside supposedly helped against the wetness outside. Considerable tenacity was required for success, so they would sometimes be at it for several days and nights. It was probably on one such occasion that someone ripped the stubborn barometer off the wall and stomped up and down on it, shouting, "I'll make you rise yet, you fiend!"

Now I slipped down the stairs and pointed my flashlight at the passage, the slaughter room, and the Octagon. Father Jesko's question had caught me like a barb that I could not get free of; I kept trying to figure out where the silver should be hidden. Probably in the slaughter room: there the floor consisted of unmortared bricks that would be easy to pry up and then replace when one had dug a hole underneath.

But I took care not to mention my exploratory mission to anyone. We had an unspoken agreement not to talk about what might befall us. Preserving our dignity, doing what each day required, not giving in to fear: "Calm is now the citizen's first duty; I challenge the citizens of Berlin to display it," read an often quoted Prussian declaration of 1806, issued after the lost battle of Jena. If we talked now, we would reveal our secret anxieties and burden others with them, and that would not be proper.

This belated triumph of Prussian upbringing was compounded by something else, probably the decisive factor: the recognition that there was nothing we could do. Any opportunity to act, however small, lends wings to our thinking, our imagination, our actions. But helplessness paralyzes. It turns the future into an insuperable wall with a grimly bolted gate. No one knows what lurks behind that wall, and no one can say what will happen when that gate finally swings open.

So, as was proper, life went on, following the natural cycle of the year. In December, with snow in the air, Father and the forester Drambusch set about planning the hunt. It could not be on such a large scale as in peacetime—too few hunters were available, for one thing. But as if on signal, Jobst arrived, now promoted to major and granted a convalescent leave "until further notice" because of his headaches and asthma attacks. His disabilities had not dimmed his enthusiasm for the hunt, and to please me he even agreed not to wear his uniform. In any case, Rumbske was not exactly thronged with soldiers needing to be kept in line. Father proved as resourceful as ever: my brother Christian was now stationed in Stolp as a recruit, and Father managed to get permission for him to sneak away from his unit for a day or two by inviting his squadron commander as well. Luckily we had no shortage of hunting rifles.

But no amount of activity could prevent the daily Wehrmacht reports from taking on new significance. The entire household would gather around the wireless in the afternoon, when the report was read and then repeated, the second time slowly enough to be written down. We listened nervously, trying to fathom the reality behind the words.

At 5:30 on the morning of December 16, following a short, intense barrage of gunfire, a powerful German force advanced from the Siegfried Line in a broad formation and quickly overran advanced American positions between the Hoher Venn and the northern section of Luxembourg. The major offensive continues, with strong air support. The enemy has been taken completely by surprise; to maintain this advantage, further details will not be released at this time. In air combat above the front, our fighter squadrons have shot down 48 enemy bombers, according to reports received thus far. The Luftwaffe's antiaircraft guns have brought down another 21 enemy planes. Last night our infantry and night-attack units disrupted enemy troop movements and attacked supply bases. Along the rest of the western front . . .[3]

"It's the miracle we've all been waiting for, the turning point at last!" the credulous Aunt Deten rejoiced. "Our glorious new weapons! And the Führer—"

"Will you shut up!" Father's voice sounded quiet, but the words cut like knives. His face was grim and set—a mask I had never seen before. "Do you know what this really means? The Führer is burning up all his remaining resources in the west. And when the Russians launch their great winter offensive . . ." A short pause; now everyone in the room looked grim. "As for what comes next, my dear madam, you can look it up in your Bible: the Gospel According to Saint Matthew, Chapter Twenty-four, verse twenty."

Of course no one would admit to it, but each of us secretly looked up the passage later: "But pray ye that your flight be not in the winter, neither on the sabbath day." I also read the preceding verse: "And woe unto them that are with child, and to them that give suck in those days!"

A breach in the wall, a pounding at the gate, but for a moment only.

The fragrance of gingerbread wafted through the house. As was proper, the Christmas tree was set up in the library, with the crèche in front of it: Mary and Joseph with the baby, and behind them the ox and the donkey in the stable, "because there was no room for them in the inn." Over the stable floated the multitudes of the heavenly host—wax angels attached to the branches of the Christmas tree; they would melt if they came near a candle flame. Caspar, Melchior, and Balthazar were already approaching from afar. Most prominent of all, however, were the shepherds with their flocks; one carried a lamb on his shoulder.

When I was little, I always puzzled over those shepherds. The nativity landscape was covered with green moss, but in our Pomeranian climate it did not take much imagination to see the pastures deep in snow. Why would the herds be out of doors at this time of year? "A sheep can eat sand but not snow," one of our proverbs said. That meant it would find something to eat even in fields that looked completely bare to us after the hay rake had collected every last blade; but in winter sheep needed to be fed and sheltered. And why were the shepherds out with their flocks "by night"? Perhaps they did not want to be seen, because they had their sheep in the landowner's pasture. That would at least have explained why they were sore afraid when the glory of the Lord began to shine round about them.

On Christmas Eve we drove into Glowitz for the midnight service. The church was packed. As always, the confirmation class and the catechumens sat up front; to them fell the task of reciting sayings from the prophets and then lighting the candles on the Christmas tree. The manorial families occupied their special pews above the congregation. Great-Uncle Gerhard, the old Glowitzer; Frau von Bonin from Schorin; the Kepplers from Zemmin; and all the others: we nodded to one another. In the nave below, a new arrangement had been instituted. In the old days, men and women sat on different sides of the aisle. But now that the flood of refugees had brought us so many more women, and there were so few men, this principle had been abandoned; women now occupied places denied them from time immemorial.

"And the angel said unto them, Fear not: for behold, I bring you good tidings of great joy . . ." The pastor seemed to speak those words with particular emphasis today. And the congregation echoed the message with the old carol:

O you joyous
O you blessed
Mercy-bringing Christmastide.
World was forlorn,
Jesus now is born,
Rejoice, oh, rejoice
With Christian pride.

A chorus of trumpets from the church tower played the voluntary. Here, too, women had assumed new roles. They blew as powerfully as the men had once done. But why did moments like this always put me in mind of the old stories? The trumpets of Jericho:

> So the people shouted when the priests blew with the trumpets: and it came to pass, when the people heard the sound of the trumpet, and the people shouted with a great shout, that the wall fell down flat, so that the people went up into the city, every man straight before him, and they took the city.
>
> And they utterly destroyed all that was in the city, both man and woman, young and old, and ox, and sheep, and ass, with the edge of the sword.

Blitzkrieg,
If There Ever Was One

As a result of our counterassaults, the force of the enemy's attacks in the Ardennes has greatly diminished. Northeast of Laroche, our troops beat back, partly in night skirmishes, the enemy, who had made sporadic advances. In the combat zone southeast of Bastogne, the Americans were forced back by our counterassaults; a breach in the front has been closed.

Near Hatten and Rittershofen in Alsace, our mopping up of the Maginot Line fortifications continues. Attempting all day to mount a counterattack, the Americans suffered numerous and bloody casualties in the face of our concerted fire.

South of Erstein, our troops have surrounded and destroyed a second enemy battle group. In addition to the 450 recorded dead, the enemy lost at least 26 officers and 700 enlisted men who were taken prisoner, as well as considerable seized materiel.

Adverse weather conditions in central Italy have limited military activity. The British have made a few futile forays along the Adriatic coast.

In Hungary yesterday, there were only isolated skirmishes between Lake Platte and the Danube. The enemy launched fierce attacks on the southeastern section of Budapest, but these were repulsed by the garrison in heavy fighting. To the north of the Danube, our attacks achieved further success, in spite of stiffened enemy resistance. Soviet attempts to cut off our spearheads with flank attacks proved unsuccessful. Along the southern border of Slovakia, attempts by several Bolshevik infantry divisions to break through between Losoncz and the Hernad River were thwarted.

The long-awaited Bolshevik winter offensive along the Vistula has begun. Following an unusually heavy artillery bombardment, the enemy first advanced along the western front of the Baranów bridgehead with numerous infantry divisions and tank brigades. Intense fighting is raging. . . .[4]

The beginning and middle sections of the Wehrmacht report of January 13, 1945 sounded almost reassuring. All sorts of developments were listed before any mention was made of the great offensive that had begun the previous day along the Vistula. And even that was "long-awaited," which implied that defensive measures had been carefully prepared.

Within a few days, everything changed: snowstorms, hard frost, and then, in a biting east wind, a "blitzkrieg" if there ever was one. By January 20 we were hearing not about remote parts of Poland but about the "crucial battle for the German eastern territories." The enemy was advancing inexorably into East Prussia and Silesia; suddenly the towns referred to in the dispatches had familiar names like Gumbinnen, Allenstein, Oppeln. And still the Russians kept coming.

A trek of refugees passed on the highway to Stolp, then another, and another. Soon the gray column became uninterrupted: women, children, and old people, fleeing west toward the Oder. Who knew where the journey would take them; they were willing to try anything to save themselves from the sinister wave sweeping in from the east. But progress was painfully slow, the column repeatedly grinding to a halt. The carts had been loaded in haste and were often off balance; often too few horses were pulling them. Axles and wheels were forever breaking. The horses were exhausted.

They often lost their footing on the city roads, and getting them up was difficult. Sometimes we saw oxen; the blood from their sore hooves stained the snow.

At nightfall gendarmes directed all the treks off the roads and into the villages. The roads were reserved for nighttime troop movements—of which there were precious few. Father Jesko, now constantly wearing his major's uniform to gain respect, took measures to provide shelter for people and animals. For instance, he banished the foals to some outbuildings in Rowen, thereby freeing up a whole stable. In the great hall of the manor, scene of so many celebrations, straw was spread to create a dormitory for thirty, forty, or even more. Marie, the cook, was put in charge of a bevy of women; all day long they peeled potatoes and stirred huge cauldrons of nourishing soup for all comers.

Pigs were slaughtered for the pot too. This measure resulted in a memorable exchange that I happened to witness. A short, paunchy fellow in a brown Party uniform came barging into the house, planted himself in front of Father Jesko, and put his hands officiously on his hips. Staring up at Father, who towered above him, he barked, "Baron, I've heard that you're slaughtering here. You can't do that—it's strictly prohibited, and I forbid it! Otherwise I'll have to report you for illegal slaughtering!"

Father gazed down at him. "Are you out of your mind? Do you want us to let these refugees starve? They need all the strength they can get."

"But the regulations! Orders! I would think you, as an officer, as a major—"

"Now listen to me, you stickler for regulations. . . ." The next words were spoken in a low, menacing tone: "Let me tell you a story. At the battle of Königgrätz, a major did something stupid, and justified himself later by saying he was just following orders. The reply he got was: 'Sir, that's why the king of Prussia made you a field officer in the first place, so you would know when *not* to carry out an order!' and now"—a sudden switch from the low tone to a parade-ground bellow—"see to it that you get out of my house and off my land! This instant! Or I'll have you slaughtered!" The paunchy fellow turned pale, beat a hasty retreat, and was never seen again.

Another visitor, on the other hand, made a very favorable impression. Late one night, when the daily turmoil seemed under control, we heard a rap on the door, and a man in a fur coat entered, calm and dignified in manner, very courteous. He introduced himself: "Dohna is the name. Please pardon the intrusion. Might I be put up for the night?"

Actually the house was long since full. But his courtesy was contagious. Mother did not hesitate. "But of course; we'd be delighted. Jesko, you'll have to give up your dressing room for tonight. Frieda, show our guest upstairs."

A smile, a slight bow. "Thank you so much. But forgive me, please: my people and my horses must be tended to first." When that, too, had been taken care of, we passed an almost merry evening together. Red wine was served, and a fire burned in the fireplace. As anecdotes were exchanged, they occasioned much laughter. We spoke of many things, but not of the precariousness of our present circumstances.

Our Major

The men were called up. First Jobst received the telegram, expected by now, that ordered him to rejoin his unit. Apparently his headaches and his asthma no longer counted. I went with him as far as Stolp; the local railway was still running as usual.

Or rather, not quite as usual: a car had been coupled to the locomotive, and the American POWs from Rowen were loaded into it. They were laughing and cheering and singing. And who could blame them? It was obvious that this was the first stage on the road to liberation and, eventually, home. Shortly afterward the Russian POWs were withdrawn from Zedlin, though they had to go on foot.

Now only the French were left.

In Stolp, Jobst and I spent the night at the Franciscan.

Not the finest hotel in town, but it had the distinction of having housed Field Marshal von Mackensen, the old hussar. We were joined for supper by my brother, who had been given a few hours' leave. His training unit had also been placed on alert and would be moving out the following night. I tried to ring up Mother to tell her, but the telephone lines were blocked. Not until my return to Rumbske the following afternoon could I give her the bad news. Mother set out at once; she had to see her youngest and last remaining son one more time. But the evening train arrived behind schedule, and as Mother was crossing town in the unlit tram, the cavalry had already mounted and ridden off.

The last to go, the seventeen-year-olds. When Frederick the Great's war ended in 1763, the first hussars returned to Stolp with their celebrated General Belling, whose tomb lay in the Church of Saint Mary. A man as devout as he was impecunious, Belling used to pray, "You see, O Heavenly Father, the sorry straits in which Your loyal servant finds himself; please send him soon a nice little war, that he may improve his circumstances and continue to bless your name. Amen."

Luckily God turned a deaf ear to that plea. Then there was Belling's still more celebrated successor, whose monument stood guard over the marketplace: Blücher, old "Marshal Forward," hero of the Napoleonic Wars. The Belle Alliance, Blücher and Wellington, Prussians and British at Waterloo—how long ago that all seemed. And now the cavalry had ridden out of Stolp again, mere children, too young to die.

But is one ever the right age to die?

It was a crackling cold winter's day when I said goodbye to Jobst at the station, one of those farewells where one is torn between wanting to prolong it as long as possible and wanting it to be over with. While we waited for his train, a freight pulled in, its cars jammed with people. What a sight! Huddled shapes, rigid with cold, barely able to stand up anymore and climb out; thin clothing, mostly in tatters, a few blankets over bowed shoulders; gray, hollow faces. Condemned and mute; hardly a word was spoken. Aides collected stiff little bundles from among them and laid them out on the platform: children, frozen to death. The silence was broken by the cries of a mother who did not want to surrender what she had lost.

Horror and panic overcame me. Never had I seen such misery. And behind this sight, a compelling vision loomed up: These were us; this was what was in store for us; that was how it would be when the dark gate to the future was unbolted.

I was trembling all over; my legs would barely support me. Sobs shook my body. Jobst wanted to calm me; he took me in his arms—to no avail. He shouted; "Be quiet! Pull yourself together!" Finally he slapped me in the face—and that at least helped. Then his train was ready to depart. As I followed it with my eyes, I heard the signal man in his red-cap say to another railway employee, "There goes the last regularly scheduled train. There won't be any more."

A couple of days later, Father Jesko was also called up. The Volkssturm had been mobilized, and he had been put in command of five thousand older men and young boys from Stolp and the surrounding area. Children and graybeards against Soviet tanks . . .

At least we had become quite competent at coping with the nightly influx of refugees from the treks. In Rowen, Chief Inspector Hesselbarth, and in Rumbske, the steward Dargusch, had been put in charge of assigning them to quarters. (Both men were well along in years—seventy-eight and eighty-one respectively.) We women looked after the people, and our French workers took care of the horses.

But what to do on the long winter evenings, after the day's work was finished? How could we keep gloom in check, distract ourselves? The old games—skat, bridge, gin rummy, mah-jongg—proved ineffective, and no one was really in a mood to tell stories. Even Uncle Biedermann, usually full of good ideas, failed us. But his wife, Aunt Deten, had a suggestion: "How about a séance? We could summon a spirit and question it. It might have something important to tell us."

Mother straightaway put on her stern and forbidding expression, as if to say, "That's not proper; I won't have it." I felt uneasy myself; wasn't it all hocus-pocus, pure superstition? And if it wasn't, what were we getting ourselves into?

But Mother went to bed earlier than usual, with an upset stomach. And then, whether because the rest were like schoolchildren with the teacher out of the room, or because none of us could think of anything better, or because in our hopelessness and fear we were ready to clutch at straws—for whatever reason, the séance took place.

We sat around the big table in the library, resting our hands on it, our thumbs touching each other and our little fingers touching those of the people sitting next to us. A single candle, placed quite far away, shed a dim light. Aunt Deten muttered something incomprehensible, and then, in the quiet wailing or moaning voice one associates with spirits, she said, "Ghost, O ghost, are you there? Ghost, can you hear us?"

A pause, and she said it again, and again. Nothing happened. Then suddenly, unexpectedly, the table moved. A tapping. How could that be? The table was solid oak, and massively heavy. Even standing up, you would have needed a lot of strength to lift it.

"Ghost, O ghost, to whom do you wish to speak?" Tapping, while we feverishly counted the letters: J . . . O . . . B . . . S . . . T. Jobst! "Ghost, O ghost, what is your message for him?" More tapping: "His . . . helmet . . . tighter."

"No, no! Stop! That's enough! This is madness!" I jumped up, switched on the light to put an end to the nightmare. But that turned out not to be so easy. The uncanny had taken hold; it poisoned the night, disturbing sleep. What had happened? How was it to be interpreted?

Not until years later did I finally hold the official notification in my hands: Major Jobst-Werner Adam, Baron Oldershausen, was ordered to the defense of Küstrin. A couple of weeks after our ill-omened session, on March 12, 1945, he met his death within the ancient walls of the Prussian fortress there.

After nine days away, Father Jesko suddenly reappeared, exhausted and extremely downcast. He took off his uniform and did not put it on again. It was hard to get anything out of him, even later, when he had recovered somewhat. But the farmers and estate hands who had gone with him proved all too eager to talk. They needed to get the experience off their chests. As so often with eyewitness accounts, the versions contradicted each other, sometimes sharply, but this much could be gleaned:

The entire Volkssturm was loaded in Stolp onto an enormously long train. It headed south, through Rummelsburg toward Schneidemühl. Only "our major" and a few other officers had uniforms, and they had brought their own revolvers. The others had only armbands. But they had stuffed their rucksacks with provisions, and as was proper for the Pomeranian winter, they were all warmly dressed and had on stout boots, "except for the couple of townsfolk, who didn't have a clue about nothin'." The train made very slow progress because the tracks were frequently blocked by oncoming trains filled with refugees. "No, no—it was because they didn't have no idea where they wanted us!" Somewhere along the way they saw a smart parlor car on a siding; in it sat the commander of the Vistula army group, Heinrich Himmler. The major was summoned on board. He was told, and he passed it on to the men, that the Volkssturm would receive their weapons in Schneidemühl.

But well before they got there, the trip suddenly ended. Russian tanks fired on the train, fortunately from some way off and without hitting it. The railwaymen uncoupled their locomotive and took off, and the passengers scrambled out of the carriages and ran. In a hollow sheltered by woods, the major assembled his men and ordered them to march back to Stolp. The roads were blocked by the treks, so their route took them mainly across country, through snow at least knee-deep and sometimes waist-deep. The major put together groups of stronger men and assigned to them the job of breaking a path for the rest of the five thousand to follow. Each lead group was relieved after half an hour. In this fashion they proceeded without incident, resting in the woods for only a couple of hours at a time. They lit large fires to keep warm.

At last they reached Stolp. With the exception of one farmer, who had a gun or revolver and turned it on himself, they suffered no casualties. The major lined up the men on Stephansplatz, in front of the city hall, and made a brief speech: "We will defend our homeland when the Wehrmacht calls upon us to do so, but not like this; like proper soldiers. Until then, you should all go home!" He gave them a real military salute, "a proper one, for a soldier, not one of Adolf's." The major did not get away all that quickly, however; a couple of thousand men wanted to shake his hand.

At first these reports alarmed me: insubordination, undermining military preparedness, or whatever the standard slogans were—I was sure all kinds of things could be made of the episode. What would the Nazis in Stolp report to the Gauleiter in Stettin, and what brutal responses and instructions would issue from there? But again and again I was told, "Oh, my lady, don't you worry your head about nothin'! If they want to get our major, there'll be a *real* Volkssturm in Stolp. And besides, who've they got left? Ex-Party members, that's who! No sticking by the Nazis on that march, all the badges torn off and dropped in the snow. By the time we got back to Stolp, there weren't none left. . . ."

That had probably been Father Jesko's last tour of duty as a soldier—and quite possibly his finest.

Once, when we were alone together, I asked him, "Why aren't you proud of what you did? And why aren't you wearing your uniform anymore?"

A sad expression, a strangely chastened reply, Prussia's swan song: "The uniform? Oh, Libussa, it's been dishonored by those Hitlers and those Himmlers."

A Last Chance

On the lower Oder, military activity on both sides remained confined to mutual reconnaissance. North of Arnswalde, the Bolsheviks have pushed on from the Ihna bridgeheads captured yesterday, advancing into our main combat zone.

Along the flanks of the enemy's incursion into East Pomerania, intense fighting by our armored forces yesterday succeeded in preventing further enemy penetration. Seventy-two Soviet tanks were destroyed. South of Rummelsburg, we retook lost territory in a counterattack. Enemy tank spearheads pushed northwest along a narrow corridor, reaching the Köslin-Schlawe highway.[5]

None of us really listened to the rest of the Wehrmacht report. The Köslin-Schlawe highway! That road ran along close to the Baltic coast. Father Jesko circled it on the map: barely fifteen kilometers. Not even that far to the lakes of Buckow and Jamund, and beyond them was no decent road. Besides, we knew that the official reports lagged behind reality. That meant, to put it in the most sober and chilling terms, that the escape route to the west was cut off.

The treks became bewildered. Many of them were still heading west. Those already on the road had little access to news reports, and what they did hear they could not interpret without maps and a knowledge of the terrain. The Party headquarters and other authorities were, if anything, even more bewildered, to the extent that they were not already dissolving. No one wanted to make decisions or issue orders that might suggest they had a crisis on their hands. The fear of being accused of starting a panic and of being shot or hanged for defeatism made those responsible—or rather, those irresponsible—lag even further behind reality than the Wehrmacht reports.

To have the enemy approaching not from the east but from the west, making all those laboriously dug trenches utterly useless—that did not fit with any of the plans probably even now sitting in various official safes.

So while some of the treks continued to head west, others turned north toward the coast, in hopes of being picked up by ships at Stolpmünde or Leba. Still others, and in numbers that grew by the hour, turned back east. Their new destinations were Danzig and Gotenhafen.

And what about us; what could we do? When we conferred, Chief Inspector Hesselbarth reported, "The people don't want to leave. They think there's no point anymore. They want to stay home. Here they know what's what and can manage. I'm inclined to agree with them. My wife and I are also staying put. But you, Baron and Baroness—I've served your family for three generations, in keeping with our Pomeranian saying 'Steadfast in loyalty.' And therefore I advise you, from the bottom of my heart: Don't stay here! You must get out, at any cost! You're the owners of the estate and the manor, not little folk like us. And when the Russians come marching in . . . I mean, you know . . ." The old man could not finish; his voice was choked with tears.

So there would be no trek from the estate, neither westward nor in any other direction. Father Jesko's general-staff outlines ended up in the wastebasket: sketches of routes with possible intermediate destinations, lists of the holdings of friends, relatives, and acquaintances where we might rest and catch our breath. All that remained to organize was the departure of the "manor folk," as the villagers called us, or, put more drastically and more to the point: the attempt to flee in the two carriages, with a wagon for the baggage. The cartwright built a roof frame for the wagon, and the carpet from the library was laid over it. They placed a mattress inside for me, already in my ninth month.

The candidates for flight assembled in the study, beneath the painting of Frederick the Great and the antlers and hunting trophies. Besides Father Jesko, Mother, and me, there was Fräulein Rahn, the housekeeper, Uncle Biedermann and Aunt Deten from Berlin, Fräulein Trautmann from Wuppertal, Frieda the chambermaid, and Marie, our faithful cook, who had been part of the household for ages. Nine persons in all.

Father showed us the escape route to the east, on back roads that hugged the coast. To buck us up, he said, "As the crow flies, it's only fifty kilometers to the spit of land between the Baltic and Lake Zarnowitz. There, if anywhere, the defenses for the Bay of Danzig will have been positioned. It's the only line they can hold. That will give us time to get to the ships, either in Gotenhafen or in Hela. And a couple of kilometers beyond Lake Zarnowitz is Krockow; we can stop and rest with our relatives there."

Instructions followed, the old soldier once more in his element: "Don't take more than you can carry: a suitcase in each hand and a rucksack! No ship will accept anyone with more than that. The most important things go in the rucksack: jewels, valuables, papers, a change of clothing. You can't carry suitcases very far, and we may have to leave them behind at some point. But you can walk with a rucksack. Any questions?"

Marie had several: "Baron, what should we take to eat? I have a barrel of salt pork. And flour, so we can bake. A big sack of sugar. And another of coffee beans. Also—"

"No, no, that can't be done; it's too much. Every unnecessary item will make travel more difficult. Iron rations will do just fine. In two or three days we'll either be in Krockow, where we can pick up fresh provisions, or . . . Well, in either case we won't need all that."

The cook refused to allow her resolve to be shaken. Keeping us comfortable and fed was her mission in life: "Baron, a person has to eat."

"No, no, I refuse to permit it."

A ripple of laughter, even at a moment like this.

"I mean, bread, of course, and some sausages. A ham, if you like. And thermos bottles. But not all those boxes and barrels and sacks; absolutely not. The roads will probably be muddy; the horses will need all their strength, and the sacks of oats will weigh enough as it is."

Marie did not reply, and as later became clear, she came

out the clear winner in her battle against masculine stubbornness. While the wagon was waiting in the barn, she secretly loaded her provisions, hiding them under the straw.

But who would drive us? We could not expect men of the village to leave their families. Karl Pallas, though, a grizzled, hard-drinking man, declared; "It's a matter of honor! I always drove their lordships, and now I'm supposed to leave them in the lurch? Coachman is what I am, and coachman is what I'll stay."

It was splendid of him, but he was still only one man, and we had three conveyances. Of course, Father Jesko could take a pair of reins, although it would be better for him to be able to move around. But we were still one short. Father decided to talk to Pierre. He was one of the French POWs and had been working for years with the foals and as a substitute coachman. We called him "Horse Pierre," to distinguish him from "Garden Pierre." Father asked me to go with him, because my French was better, and for this delicate mission everyday basic communication in Pomeranian Low German might not be sufficient.

The conversation was very short. Pierre immediately agreed to go with us into the unknown, although we insisted, "It's up to you; we're just asking a favor. If you'd rather stay with your comrades . . ." With a smile and a slight bow, Pierre turned to me and said, *"Je ne fais que mon devoir, madame."*

Naturally, word got around, with unexpected results. Karl Peske and Walter Kreft turned up; loath to be put to shame, they now wanted to come too. All at once we had four drivers when we needed only three. Should we ask Pierre to stay behind after all? "No," Father Jesko decided. "Every additional man will be a help."

So we were ready to leave. But we could not go yet; we had to wait for our evacuation orders, or at least authorization for a trek. Anything not expressly authorized remained strictly prohibited. If anything was still functioning, it was the implacable system of control: without a stamped piece of paper, we would never get past the next crossroads, where the gendarmes, the Wehrmacht MPs, and the SS commandos all appeared to be multiplying, while fighting troops were few and far between. The thinking seemed to be that if you could not stop the enemy, at least you could stop your own people.

Now we waited, for days and nights, while precious time was lost. In the midst of this waiting, we were sitting at lunch one day when a motorcycle roared up to the house. No, it was not the courier with our authorization but, completely unexpectedly, a man in a blue naval officer's uniform—Viktor Howaldt, a friend from better days in Berlin, sailing parties on the Wannsee . . . We hugged each other.

"Vicky, whatever brings you here?"

"I've come from Leba to get you."

He had a flotilla of PT boats under his command, and it had just put into the small Baltic harbor almost around the corner from us. And at dusk they were setting off toward the west.

"Of course, there are some risks. We have to worry about mines and Russian subs, and perhaps low-flying aircraft. But our chances of making it through are good, much better than with any other type of vessel. We're fast and maneuverable, we can change course or defend ourselves. So bundle up, Libussa, and hop on! We'll be in Leba and and on board in an hour."

Mother was horrified: "Dear Herr Howaldt, just look at my daughter! She's due in three weeks. You expect her to ride that motorcycle of yours, with the roads all potholes and stones? Absolutely not!"

"Very well, then, hitch up the fastest horses you have. If they go all out, we can still make it. I'll escort you through the checkpoints. Don't forget, madam, this may be her last chance."

He was right; I sensed that. This opportunity to get out was a sign, truly a last chance. Yet something inside me resisted. I also sensed that if I left my parents now, I would never see them again. They would never survive on their own; they would need me, if only to have someone to live for.

Who can say what motivates us at times like this? In my case, it certainly was not courage, more likely fear—the fear of not being able to forgive myself someday. I heard myself saying, "Dear Viktor, I'll never forget your doing this for me. But please understand: I can't leave. I have to stay here."

A quick hug, and farewells. The motorcycle roared off.

To Zackenzin and Back

"Comment allez-vous?
How's things, madame?"

Violent pounding on the door startled me out of restless sleep. I heard shouting: "Trek orders! Get up! Hurry! We're leaving as soon as possible!" Trek orders . . . It was the night of March 8, 1945, still very dark outside. As I rushed to get dressed, Frieda appeared, to take my suitcase downstairs.

Soon we were all assembled; the hall looked like a railway station, with all our luggage piled up. Breakfast was served. "Do me a favor and eat!" Father Jesko ordered, and added, "We won't be having any lunch." But hardly anyone felt like eating; we just fortified ourselves with coffee. No one was in a mood to talk, either.

In the meantime, Marie dragged in those of her provisions that were not already stowed away: a laundry basket full of sandwiches and thermos bottles, another with bread, a third with hams, sausages, canned goods, and more and more. . . . Father stared at her disapprovingly. He took a canning jar, pulled off the lid, and shook the jellied meat out onto the carpet. Then he whistled for Faust, our hound, and pointed out the treat. The dog happily fell to.

A scene without words, but I was sure I was not the only

one whose heart was pierced by it. That carpet was magnificent, the pride of the house. We always gasped when someone seemed about to step on it in anything but spotless shoes. Probably no one ever did. Now the dog was eating off it. No words could have stated it with such pitiless eloquence: it was all over now, forever.

The front door stood open, and we could hear the sound of wheels and hooves outside; the carriages were rolling up the drive. It would take a few minutes for the baggage to be loaded. I slipped up to my room, closed the door, leaned against the wall, and took a few last breaths, a last look around, saying goodbye.

The door was cautiously pushed open. Two women tiptoed in, two of the evacuees from the west who had been lodged with us. "Over there, the wardrobe," one of them whispered.

"Will you kindly wait until we're gone! You'll have plenty of time for looting."

The women spun around, stared at me. Greed distorted their faces, and rage at being caught. They slunk out as quietly as they had come in.

We set off, with just the first hint of light showing in the eastern sky. I lay on my mattress, provided with pillows and a fur travel rug, above me the carpet roof. "My mattress grave," I thought. Wasn't it Heine, a German poet, who coined that phrase as he lay dying in a foreign land? Marie and Frieda kept me company in the wagon. Pierre, our coachman, often turned and smiled at me encouragingly: *"Comment allez-vous?"* Or, in the wonderful mixture of his native tongue with Pomeranian Low German, the result of his five years with us, "How's things, *madame?*" Someone else seemed concerned about me too: Faust. Whenever the procession stopped and he got bored with circling the vehicles, he would jump into my wagon, lick my hands, and gaze into my eyes: "How's things?"

We drove past Rowen to Glowitz, then north along the great moor, past Zemmin to Giesebitz and Lake Leba. There we turned east. But progress was slow, pitifully slow. The roads were in terrible shape. The mud season had arrived: frost heaves, deep potholes, ruts everywhere, full of icy water. The horses were strong and well rested, and Father Jesko's forethought in not letting us load ourselves down with all sorts of unnecessary things should have been paying off now. But so many people were on the move with us, all too many; this could hardly be called a forgotten back road. Far too many had hopelessly overloaded their wagons. Some had been wandering around for weeks, and their teams were tired and lame. There was no way to get past them. When night fell, the gendarmes appeared, to do their duty and clear the road for military traffic—of which there was so sign. We were directed to a small estate.

"How much ground did we cover?" I asked Father, as we got down and stretched our legs.

He looked around to make sure no one was listening. "Not enough," he replied softly.

To the extent possible, the crowd of refugees was put up in the manor house. Every available room had been turned into a dormitory, with straw to sleep on, but Mother and I were given a small room to ourselves, with two beds. The kitchen was abuzz with activity; from the bubbling cauldrons we could all eat our fill. But the surprise of the evening was provided by Pierre: he brought me a cup of hot cocoa. We had not had anything like that for a long time; it must have come from a Red Cross parcel for the POWs.

We felt almost safe here—almost. In our quiet bedroom we noticed a faint rattling of the window. I opened it and heard distant thunder, like a summer storm approaching. The reflection of lightning appeared in the sky. But it was not summer yet, and the storm was man-made.

The next morning we set out as early as possible, even before daybreak. But so did all the others. Everyone was trying to steal a march on the rest, so no one gained any advantage. Our progress proved even more halting than the day before. We had to cross the Lauenburg-Leba highway, which was crowded with treks heading north to the coast. But Leba, long since overcrowded, had been sealed off; the northward stream had been diverted to the east, onto our road.

That evening we reached Zackenzin, another day's journey away from the possibility of safety in the narrows before Danzig. This time we had no need to wait for the stillness of night to hear the thunder rumbling. Tanks against horses: an uneven race. We flinched at the roar of the guns and the exploding shells. In the west, the dying light flared with torches that would illuminate the night: farms or entire villages ablaze.

Another night in a manor house; again Mother and I were given beds, while all the rest lay on straw. Again Pierre brought me a cup of deliciously fragrant hot chocolate. But the mood had changed. Yesterday there was still hustle and bustle, nourished by the hope that with a bit of luck we could get through. One heard a din of voices, and even laughter now and then. Today everyone was whispering. The fear of impending disaster had gripped us all. What would the next day bring?

Ancient, long-forgotten childhood fears reappeared: fear of the dark, fear of falling asleep. Childhood memories of hide-and-seek, nursery rhymes:

Ladybug, ladybug, flee far away,
Your father's at war and not to be found.
Your mother's in Pomeraniay,
Alas, Pomerania's burned to the ground.

But then—sheer exhaustion—sleep came after all.

The Turning Point

"Libussa, wake up!" Someone was shaking my shoulder.

A flashlight was shining on me, blinding me. "What time is it? Is it time to go?"

"Ssh! Yes, it's time. Get up, we're going out to the park."

Someone lit a candle. I heard a clock strike the hour. I saw my mother sitting on her bed and made out Father Jesko. He was wearing his uniform, with all his medals and ribbons from two world wars. Was I dreaming?

No. Suddenly I was wide awake and knew exactly what was happening: If there was no hope of escape, we were going to commit suicide. We had pistols with us, and they would perform this last service for us. It was something we had never discussed, never stated unambiguously, probably never even thought through to the end, but the moment had now come.

Or had we discussed it? Yes, at least once, months earlier, in the fall, when terrifying reports and photographs from the East Prussian border were passed around, and one place name, the site of particular atrocities, kept cropping up: Nemmersdorf. At the time we had said we had to make sure we didn't go through that. Since then, especially in the last few weeks, refugee accounts and hints from soldiers had confirmed repeatedly that the tales of horror were neither fantasy nor propaganda but fact.

Father said again, "It's time. The Russians will be here in an hour, two at most."

"But what if we set out right now?" I ventured.

"Out of the question. We wouldn't make it—they're so much faster. And to be caught on the road would be worst of all."

We had to make sure we didn't go through that; at such times, everything seems perfectly clear. There are no misunderstandings, no persuasion is necessary, no words need be spoken. The situation itself dictates what must be done. Now this was our only way out. Back in the fall, we had first set foot on this path. Now we took each other's hands to follow it to the end.

But as we reached the threshold, an insuperable barrier suddenly loomed ahead of me: the situation had changed since that time six months before.

"Mother, wait, please, I can't do it."

"Don't be afraid, child, it will be quick and painless. Remember the inscription on our cross back home: 'Fear not, but trust in the Lord.' "

"No, no, it isn't that. I'm not afraid. I want to go with you, but I can't. I'm carrying the baby, my baby. It's kicking so hard. It wants to live. I can't kill it."

A deep sigh. "Are you quite sure?"

"Yes, Mother."

Her hand squeezed mine. "Then that's how it has to be. And I'll stay with you, come what may." She took me in her arms and hugged me tight.

Father stood by, at a loss, groping for words. "But, Emmy, Mother, the two of us . . ."

"No, Jesko, no. You heard what she said. Who will help Libussa when her time comes? It's not likely a doctor or a midwife will be around."

"And what about me—what am I supposed to do?"

By now I saw the whole thing clearly. "The first thing you can do is get out of that stupid outfit and throw it in the pond, and the pistols with it! If the Russians find any of those things, we're finished!"

He stammered, "Outfit? This outfit? Libussa . . ."

"All right, your uniform. But for heaven's sake, do what I said!"

The Conquerors

Then there are all the unbelievable things that happen on the side, while we are forced to fold our arms and watch! The most brilliantly imaginative atrocity stories pale by comparison with the things perpetrated by this organized band of killers, robbers, and looters, apparently with tacit support from the top. The extermination of entire families, including women and children, can be carried out only by subhumans who no longer deserve to be called German.

I am ashamed to be a German! This minority that defiles the name of Germany by killing, burning, and looting will one day become the misfortune of the entire German people, unless we stamp out its activities very soon.[6]

Our little band of refugees, thirteen in all, assembled in one room. As we sat on the straw bedding, Father burned our identity papers in the tiled stove, so that we would not be recognized immediately as "lordships." Everything was strangely hushed. No bustle in the manor or the courtyard. But also no noise of gunfire or rattle of tanks. What was going on? I sneaked out to have a look; the waiting seemed intolerable.

In the morning light I could see young trees—a fir plantation, probably—at either side of the road that had brought us to Zackenzin. Nothing moved. But then two or three flares shot up from the edge of the plantation, and suddenly everything was transformed: engines started up with a wail, the trees moved, came crashing down, and like stone age monsters, tanks lumbered out into the open. Quick, back into the house: they were coming!

Now everything seemed to happen very quickly. In a matter of minutes the monsters rolled down the village street and clattered into the courtyard. The deafening echo of the tank guns, firing not at any enemy but to intimidate the populace or to signal victory; submachine guns; then coarse shouts, boots clattering into the house and up the stairs. The door burst open, soldiers charged into the room, and a volley of shots passed right over our heads. Plaster dust rained down.

Strange, sinister figures they were: fairly short, to a man, stooped, bandy-legged, and slant-eyed—Tatars, presumably. But most noticeable was their shabbiness, their raggedness. Quite a few of them lacked proper boots, and I noticed that instead of leather gun straps, they had only lengths of string or rope.

Odd: these men did not fit the image we always had of conquerors—tall and erect, proudly decked out, with medals and oak-leaf insignia. Notions cultivated over generations welled up, memories of newsreel footage of victory parades in Warsaw and Paris, patriotic Prussian ideals from our school days, pictures and rhymes from a children's book on Frederick the Great:

And terror sweeps the highway
Down which the armies march,
The flags flap taut with victory,
Parading toward honor's arch.

These conquerors were clearly not interested in parades but in loot. The welcoming salvo was immediately followed by shouts of *"Uri! Uri!"*—they wanted our watches. And of course the first to get there amassed the most. One soldier pushed up his sleeve to accommodate his new haul, and I saw he had almost an even dozen already. Pierre lost his watch too, even though he kept protesting *"Franzose! Franzose!"* When he tried to resist, he got a rifle butt in the ribs. Next came our luggage. The suitcases were broken open in a jiffy and greedily pawed through. Thank goodness we had had the foresight to take off our rings and earrings to avoid having them ripped off. We had hidden them in our underwear, in soap holders or rolled-up socks. But the looters were experienced and quickly found what they were looking for. One of them reached into my rucksack and with practiced hand pulled out the red leather case that held my jewelry. One of the items in it was a gold cross studded with blue turquoise, on a gold chain. In 1888, Johanna von Bismarck, wife of the founder of the German empire, gave it to Mother, who was her goddaughter, and Mother had passed it on to me; an early photograph showed me wearing the cross. The soldier slashed the leather with his knife, checked over the items, and stole a quick look at his comrades to make sure they had not noticed. Then the case with its contents disappeared into his tunic.

This first encounter with the conquerors lasted only a matter of minutes. Orders rang up from the hall below, and the whole gang galloped off again, leaving the house trembling in the roar of their tank engines. Already the metal monsters were clanking through the village, heading east along the road we had planned to travel that day.

Strange, too, how one registers such an event. One's consciousness, one's identity, seems to split. One half holds on firmly, digs in, finally withdraws deep into the recesses of the body, into the pit of the stomach or under the pounding heart, from where it responds almost automatically, literally in the flesh. Meanwhile the other half flits off and observes from a distance. It keeps very still; you are hardly aware of it, and the more dramatic events become, the more unobtrusive it gets.

But later, when the situation calms down, when, still shaking, one manages to take a few deep breaths, this second self returns to its twin, almost casually, as if to say: What are you getting all excited about? But in fact the runaway has been feverishly busy, catching and recording images. Any minute now, it will produce them. And with stubborn persistence it will dig them out time and again, whether one is waking or dreaming.

Those stooped, ragged conquerors, with their weapons held by lengths of string, for instance; the furtive glance of the jewel thief: those images were so sharp and definitive that a wholly detached photographer might have taken them. Decades have passed since then, and still they suddenly pop up before my mind's eye like pictures in an album, and with a shudder I consent to look at them: yes, that's how it was, that's how it looked—just a little while ago, almost yesterday.

We had only a brief moment to catch our breath before the next wave hit us. No roar of engines, no rattle of caterpillar tracks; this time we heard the clatter of hundreds of hooves: a cavalry unit, men on horseback. They had, or gave themselves, more time than their predecessors. They, too, were intent on booty, but in another, far worse sense. The men who now burst into our room took a quick look around. One of them pointed to Marie: "Woman, come!" She was picked up and carried off. And Marie was certainly not the only one; the house echoed with the screams of women.

How long did it go on? Eventually the screaming died down, then stopped. Marie staggered back into the room, her clothes in tatters. I took her in my arms. She tried to break away, but I held her tightly. Then she burst into tears. Cry, I thought, just cry; perhaps it will help.

In a little while a man with broad epaulets appeared, an officer. He was brandishing a pistol, and behind him two soldiers had their guns at the ready. He bawled, "Talk or I shoot! Where is lord? Where is owner?" But how could we have answered that? We heard later that the owner of the Zackenzin estate, a veterinarian, had escaped through a window with his son at the last moment and got away across the park. We also learned that before the arrival of the victorious army he had ordered the distillery's entire stock to be poured down the drain, which apparently enraged the Russians and made them intent on revenge. But who could say—perhaps it was precisely the absence of alcohol, thanks to the veterinarian's foresight, that saved our lives.

The officer went through the house, then, with a sure instinct, made his choice. He came back, planted himself in front of Father Jesko, pointed his pistol at his chest, and said simply, "You!"

Father stood up, very tall, very slim, very straight; not until he was standing was he unmistakably a "lord." The Russian gestured to him to follow.

Mother threw me a despairing look. Almost mechanically, without knowing what I was going to do, I heaved myself up and went after the men, down the stairs and out the front door. Father was standing with his back to the wall of an outbuilding. He did not see me; he was staring straight ahead. The officer was shouting orders across the courtyard, assembling a firing squad, presumably.

As quickly as I could, I ran across to Father Jesko and took up a position in front of him. I pointed to my belly, unmistakably that of a woman in her ninth month. I writhed in pain, as though I had already gone into labor. "Doctor!" I shouted repeatedly, pointing alternately at my belly and at the condemned man behind me. The officer stared at me. Was he convinced? He shook his head—and waved, twice: once to his men, to indicate they would not be needed, and once to us, to indicate we should get out of his sight. But

Father Jesko did not respond; he stood there, stiff as a board, staring into space. I grabbed his hand and pulled him after me.

"Stoi!" The officer came after us, pointing to Father's boots. "Take off!"

That at least made sense. None of these Russian cavalrymen had such elegant and beautifully cared for riding boots. I brought Father back inside in his stocking feet but otherwise unharmed. Luckily he had a pair of oxfords with him, which would have the added advantage of being less conspicuous.

Gallows Row

Two days passed, and two nights. Fresh waves of soldiers kept rolling over us, drunk with victory; the raping and looting continued. Sometimes an unexpected lull occurred, more often by day than by night. But no one knew how long it would last. Sometimes in the midst of a soldiers' rampage we would simply nod off from sheer exhaustion, only to wake with a start, full of dread.

At some point we realized Pierre was gone. What had happened to him? No one knew. His allies and liberators must have dragged him away in a hurry, for if he had had a moment, he would certainly have come to say goodbye. The half-empty can of cocoa was all we had to remember him by.

Someone else was missing: Faust, our hound. Before the Russians arrived, Father Jesko had locked him in a kennel near the manor, saying, "It's better this way. If he stays with us, he'll try to defend us, and then they'll shoot him." The precaution proved to have been in vain. In a moment when things seemed to have quieted down, I slipped out to look for him. The kennel door had been pried open. I called his name softly, but he did not answer. Then I found him, lying on the manure pile, riddled with bullets. I reported what I had seen, but no one could summon the energy to go out and bury the poor beast.

On the third day we became acquainted with a new institution: the "Kommandatura." A notice went up on the barn door, and we were all rounded up to read it. It said, in neat Gothic script: "Official instructions! Each person must return to his domicile! Anyone found out of place in three days will be punished!—The Kommandatura." Then a properly Cyrillic signature below, and even an official stamp.

The instructions certainly seemed sensible. Blown by the wind of circumstance, the flotsam and jetsam of the treks had washed up unevenly. Some villages were almost deserted, while others were spilling over with people. All these people would doubtless be better off in their own towns and villages, not to mention that the new masters would find it easier to keep track of and maintain control over them.

But carrying out the instructions turned out to be very difficult. To begin with, our horses were gone, probably taken by the cavalry unit that came after the first wave of tanks. One of our two carriages had also disappeared. What in heaven's name—or what the devil—would a modern army want with a carriage? Pallas, who had served in the First World War, had an explanation: "Well, most likely their general had a bad leg, you know. Our old Mackensen, when he had the rheumatism, he'd get down off of his horse and take the carriage."

The second carriage was still there, though in a pitiful condition, with all the seats slashed. But then we weren't going for a pleasure ride, and it was far more important that our wagon was still where we had left it. The carpet that had served as a roof was gone, but to our utter astonishment all of Marie's provisions were still there: the barrel of meat and the sacks of flour, coffee, and sugar were intact. So we could harness up and set out for home, if only we had a team. Or even just one horse.

After a long search, Pallas and Peske succeeded in rounding up an ownerless horse. Admittedly, he was terribly emaciated, and lame to boot—we promptly dubbed him Hobble. We could not expect him to have much strength, but he was better than nothing. By now it was quite late in the day, so we postponed our departure until the following morning. In the meantime, we hid Hobble behind a barn and fed him more oats than he had probably had in weeks.

We left Zackenzin, heading west toward home. I was installed on my mattress once more, though now with an unrestricted view of the sky, where clouds went scudding along, chased by a chill March wind. But I was bundled up warm, almost cozy. None of our fur coats or lap rugs had been taken; apparently the Russians had plenty of their own. Hobble was harnessed to one wagon shaft and did his utmost. But because he had so little strength, our entire group, now dwindled to twelve, had to walk and help push the wagon uphill, except me. Only Aunt Deten, almost as lame as Hobble and with three times his girth, was allowed to join me in the wagon now and then.

The road before us was deserted, and without the endless column of refugees we could make more rapid progress than we had some days earlier, going in the opposite direction with strong, well-rested horses. Branches kept passing before my eyes, some belonging to the forests along the road, others to the fine old trees planted to either side. The rhythmic crunching of the wheels and the shaking and swaying of the cart soon made me doze off.

Shouts, perhaps a scream; I woke with a start. What was happening? What fresh horror awaited us? Before my eyes, coming closer and closer, now almost above me, a figure, a corpse, dangled from a branch. He wore the uniform of the German Wehrmacht—only his boots were missing. He swayed to and fro, half twisting in the wind. His head lolled to one side. There was a faint odor of decay, and two crows flew off lazily, cawing. The sign pinned to his chest was still perfectly legible: "Here I hang because I did not believe in the Führer."

The horror was past, but not for long. Another one loomed up, with a different motto: "Traitors will die, as this one did."

A third: "He who shuns death in honor dies in dishonor."

A fourth: "I was too cowardly to fight for women and

children." But who had started the war in the first place, who was responsible for what was now being done to women and children?

Farther on, at a crossroads, two men hung side by side. This time they were gendarmes, and they had neither their boots nor signs around their necks. Probably—no, all too obviously—this was the work not of German courts-martial but of the Russians.

It went on and on, only the executioners alternating. Gallows row, a display of male frenzy, of crazed blood lust on both sides, with a horrifying similarity between victors and vanquished. The losers wanted to drag all who resisted down with them, while the winners wanted revenge. But why take revenge on ordinary traffic policemen, who merely did as they were told?

At the same time, word was given out that all the Jews in Kiev were to be relocated. In collaboration with the group staff and two commandos of the Police Regiment Southern Sector, on September 29 and 30 Special Commando 4a executed 33,771 Jews. Money, valuables, underwear, and outerwear were secured, with some assigned to the NSV to supply German nationals, the rest to the provisional government of the city for distribution among the needy. The operation itself went off smoothly. No untoward incidents occurred. The "relocation" implemented for the Jews received the full support of the populace. The fact that the Jews were liquidated is not widely known, but as past evidence suggests, it would not have aroused much opposition. The Wehrmacht likewise approved of the measures. Those Jews who are still at large, or rather, those Jews who fled and are gradually returning to the city, are receiving the appropriate treatment on a case-by-case basis. At the same time, it proved possible to apprehend a succession of NKVD officials, political commissars, and partisan leaders and deal with them.[7]

Hobble went on strike, demanding a chance to rest. I concurred; I had had enough of lying on my back, staring up into a sky from which corpses kept entering my field of vision. So while we rested and Hobble ate with a healthy appetite—unlike the rest of us—I had my mattresses rearranged so I could sit up with my back against the side of the wagon.

When we moved off, I wondered whether I had made the right choice, or whether I had gone from the frying pan into the fire. We passed a village. Was it Labenz? I did not know; I had missed the sign. At any event, it had become a ghost town, with most of the houses, barns, and stables destroyed by fire or by shelling; only the chimneys still rose from the ruins, from amid charred beams. An eerie silence hung over everything: no dogs barked, no cows mooed, no cocks crowed, no geese or ducks quacked. No humans to be seen. Nothing. Nothing at all. Only, as if to emphasize the uncanny, godforsaken feeling, a door or shutter banging in the wind.

A new kind of death row began in the village and continued for miles: wrecked wagons hastily cleared to one side, pushed into the ditch; dead horses, their legs stiff, their stomachs distended; the remains of looted baggage—bed linens, clothing, smashed crockery, cooking pots, crates and trunks. And toys: a teddy bear, a headless doll. Here a refugee column had been overtaken, sprayed with bullets, pushed over. At least the dead had been carted off and buried.

At the end of this death row, ragged figures cowering in the ditch: a woman with three small children. The children were whimpering, the woman remained mute. Mother poured each of them a cup of hot cocoa from our thermos.

Finally the woman managed to get out a few words: "May we come along? Please, the children . . ."

"Of course," Mother said. "Climb in."

"Stoi!" As we drove through a forest, a Russian soldier, submachine gun at the ready, stepped out onto the road, with a youth at his side. A sergeant or a corporal, perhaps, a short, stocky man with a broad chest. And he needed it, too, because that chest was practically studded with medals. As the children wailed in terror, the man scrambled onto the

wagon; the youth followed him and, at a gesture from the man, began to rummage through our things.

At some point the children fell silent for a moment, and in that silence Father Jesko said quietly but perfectly audibly to Pallas, "Look, Pallas, he must really have been a brave soldier. All those medals . . ."

Strangely enough, the man understood. He pulled up short, gave his companion a slap in the face, leapt off the wagon, planted himself in front of Jesko, and saluted him as if he were saluting his own general. Involuntarily, Father and Pallas responded in kind. Soldiers all.

Another round of salutes, a curt wave, and we were permitted to continue on our way.

Hobble gave us to understand that we could not expect much more of him, at least not on this day. Quite at random, we took the next turning off the road. Mother led the horse, and the men and those of the women who had any strength left pushed the wagon. It was an exhausting undertaking, because the road had been thoroughly softened up by the thaw. But finally we reached a farm and asked for shelter.

The farmer was an old man with a beautiful white beard. He greeted us calmly and cordially. "Actually," he said, "we have people everywhere already, but as long as I can make some space, we want to share what we have. Welcome." Then he shook hands with each of us in turn. When we tried to thank him, he refused to hear of it, and he sounded straightforward and completely natural: "The Bible says, 'He that receiveth you receiveth me.' "

At the Patriarch's

Verily, there was hardly any room in the "inn," which was filled to the rafters. With our arrival, the company must have swelled to well over thirty, chiefly women and children. Most of the latter had to sleep in the hayloft, above the cows and horses. And why not? The hay made a soft, warm bed; to the children, at least, it was like an adventure. My mattress bed was made up for me in a tiny room I shared with Mother. The farmer's wife even brought us feather beds. And whether it was because I was exhausted or because I felt almost safe in the house of the kindly old man with the beard, I slept deeply and soundly until late the next morning.

When I woke up, the house had obviously been abuzz with activity for a good while. In the kitchen, while some women were still cutting and spreading slices of bread for breakfast, others had already started to peel potatoes for lunch. Others had milked the cows; the children were allowed to drink all the milk they wanted. I saw one of the terrified little things we had picked up on the road swallow an entire jugful, take a deep breath, burp twice—and break out in a smile. Meanwhile the men were busy digging a second privy over near the manure pile behind the barn, because the existing one was by no means adequate for the number of people.

A while later, Marie opened her sack of flour and set about making bread. With secret pride at having been proved right in her decision to ignore male folly, she showed Father Jesko the finished product, which smelled heavenly. "Baron, a person has to eat."

Mother seized this opportunity to introduce a linguistic reform. "Please, Marie," she said, "can we drop the 'Baron' and 'Baroness' now? If a Russian happened to hear you, it would put us in terrible danger. Please try to remember."

Marie almost lost her composure. "But, Baroness, what else can I call the baron and you?"

"From now on, simply Father Jesko, or even just Father. And Mother. And *du,* please, not *Sie.*"

A deep sigh. "Well, Baroness, if you insist . . ."

What an effort to change habits not merely ingrained since childhood but expressive of an age-old order as well! Frieda, Pallas, and all the others found the adjustment just as difficult as Marie; time and again they lapsed into the old usage, or hemmed and hawed in embarrassment when they had to address us.

TO ZACKENZIN AND BACK

But Mother, more the baroness than ever now, insisted on the new dispensation. She let no error pass unreproved, and eventually the new style became established.

Once launched, Mother decided on another significant reform. Father wanted to shave off his week's growth of stubble, but Mother decreed, "You must grow a beard."

"But why? I've never worn a beard, and it doesn't become me."

"Nonsense, Jesko. First of all, it *is* becoming to you. Just look at the farmer—see how handsome a beard can be! And second, it changes you; and third, it makes you look older. That's what we need right now."

As though to prove her right, he grew a snow-white beard modeled on our host's, even though the dark hair on Jesko's head showed hardly a streak of gray.

The farmer was not only kind, he was also devout. Like a true patriarch, he gathered his guests in the hall every evening, opened his Bible, and read out loud, for instance from Paul's Epistle to the Romans:

> Be . . . rejoicing in hope; patient in tribulation; continuing instant in prayer; distributing to the necessity of saints; given to hospitality. Bless them which persecute you: bless, and curse not. Rejoice with them that do rejoice, and weep with them that weep. Be of the same mind one toward another. Mind not high things, but condescend to men of low estate. Be not wise in your own conceits. Recompense to no man evil for evil. Provide things honest in the sight of all men. If it be possible, as much as lieth in you, live peaceably with all men.

Afterward we all joined in singing a hymn and saying the Lord's Prayer.

But there was no room for illusions; we had no Noah's ark to protect us from the flood of 1945. The farm might be remote from the stream of traffic and invisible from the road, but its remoteness offered no guarantee of safety. Perhaps even the opposite: there would be no one to witness an atrocity if one occurred. So the farmer took whatever precautions he could to protect us.

First of all, every night he sent two men out to the place where the wood road to the farm branched off from the main road. They removed all hoof marks and wagon tracks, to make it look as though the path led only to the peat bog, where no one went at this time of year. The effort would be justified if it saved us from even one unwelcome visitation.

And then, in a copse along the road, he set up a listening post. From there a signal was to be sent—by waving in the daytime, by blinking a flashlight at night—the moment a troop of Russians turned down the side road. At the farm, someone was always on duty to watch for signals and sound the alarm. If it came, almost all the women ran out to the bog and hid in the bushes.

Even Fräulein Trautmann joined them—and Aunt Deten, who manifested surprising agility. One would not have thought either of them had anything to fear. Fräulein Trautmann was a good, kind person, but also, if I may say so, forbiddingly homely. As for Aunt Deten, her age should have kept her from harm.

We owed the fact that we got through those days and nights unscathed chiefly to the farmer himself. Each time a mob came galloping up to the house, bellowing wildly, for all the world like descendants of Attila or Genghis Khan, he would go out calmly to meet them. He greeted the warriors almost as cordially as he had greeted us—but in Russian. Back in August 1914 he had been captured as a soldier in the Landwehr, and during his years in Siberia he had learned the language, which he still largely retained. Usually the soldiers were so astonished that they forgot their evil intentions, and sometimes they even began to fool around like overgrown children.

Of course, they "requisitioned" things; for instance, the flocks of geese, ducks, and hens dwindled alarmingly. For that reason the poultry soon joined the womenfolk out in the bog; an enclosure was hastily built for them. Unfortunately, it turned out not to have built solidly enough to withstand the depredations of a fox.

But how long could this go on? With the passing days, this question came to obsess us. The farmer was anything but well off. Yet he continued to insist that we could stay as long as we wished.

And what about the Kommandatura's decree that anyone "out of place" would be punished? "That's the first I've heard of it," the farmer commented. "Do you see any sign around here? Besides, this is your home; you are my friends."

But we felt we could not exploit our host's hospitality much longer. In any case, departure was in the air. A family from Giesebitz had already left. Walter Kreft and Karl Peske followed. Understandably enough, they wanted to rejoin their families, now that they were not required as drivers anymore. They thought they stood a better chance on the footpaths that crisscrossed Leba Moor than with a horse and wagon on the main road.

In the end, my own condition was what determined our course of action. Mother had learned from the farmer's wife that a "wise woman" lived nearby—not exactly a certified midwife but someone who understood herbs and natural healing, had had a good deal of experience assisting with births, and presumably also with abortions. She was secretly fetched, examined me, and said, "You'll be going into labor soon. If you want to get home before that, you'll have to hurry."

So our baggage, my mattress, and Marie's provisions were loaded onto the wagon. Hobble, restored by a week of rest, was snorting with eagerness to get on the road. It was less easy for the rest of us. "And they all wept sore, and fell on Paul's neck and kissed him." Even Pallas sniffed and wiped away a tear before taking up the reins and calling, "Gee-up!"

The farmer made the sign of the cross over us: an old man with white hair and a white beard, the very image of a patriarch.

A Child Is Born

Awful pains in my back began almost as soon as we set off, and they got steadily worse. Every jolt, every bump in the road, ran through me like a knife stab.

Mother did not tell me what they meant, but her concern was obvious. She took charge, insisting on haste. "No, let's not stop yet," I heard her saying. "The horse doesn't need a rest yet. You might lend him a hand if you like!" And when a rest became unavoidable, she tried to get the party moving again after just a few minutes. When we ran into a troop of Russians, she sought out their leader at once, and I heard over and over the words "daughter . . . labor . . . baby." Mother got her way; the Russians left the wagon alone, and after a while we were allowed to continue on. Relieved, she turned to me with an encouraging smile: "Bear up, child. It won't be long. We're almost in Rowen."

Rowen. After crossing Leba Moor and passing Giesebitz, Zemmin, and Glowitz, we reached this first of our villages. Mother made another decision: "We're turning in here; there's no time to spare!" This first house we came to belonged to a run-down farm, the property of a widowed Frau Musch.

Creatures from outer space could hardly have startled and terrified Frau Musch more than our sudden appearance. One could understand her feelings; after all, we were the old "lordships," and how would the new masters react when they heard we had returned? Perhaps with murder and arson. And if they came charging in, would they bother to distinguish between the innocent common people and the gentry? But Frau Musch had no chance to verbalize her fears; she was simply overpowered by Mother's determination. "Frau Musch, just look at my daughter. The contractions have started already. We must have shelter, and this minute."

We discovered later that we probably could not have found any other accommodations anyway. The village was bursting with refugees and stranded treks; until the previous day, Frau

Musch herself had had two families staying with her. Since she could not turn us away, the only hope for Frau Musch was to banish the "lordships" to the attic. So while Marie, Frieda, the Biedermanns, and the others found quarters down below, I was pushed and pulled first up the stairs, then up rickety steps to the attic. There were two little rooms—or rather storage areas—in the attic. They bedded me down on my mattress in one of them, while Mother and Father Jesko occupied the other.

It was the evening of March 21. In the tradition of Pierre, Marie brought me a cup of hot cocoa, with instructions to enjoy it; this was absolutely the last of our French supply—"not a speck left." Alas, I could not enjoy it very well.

During the night it seemed as though the birth were imminent. The contractions were close together now, and more severe. Frieda helped Mother look after me, for in such a situation Marie was too nervous. All she could do was bring me something to drink or renew the supply of boiling water, which kept getting cold. Frieda, on the other hand, remained calm and energetic. To keep me moving between contractions, she got me onto my feet and led me back and forth, supporting me when a contraction came.

The waves crashed, ebbed away, returned. But to no avail; there was no progress. Hours passed. As Frieda put it, for Marie's benefit when she peeped in again. "Our cart's stuck in the mud, in over both axles. Our horsey just can't manage it." An apt image, alas. Except that a horse would probably have given up, while we complicated human beings were made to persevere.

Day broke; the sun climbed in the sky, heating up the roof under which I was lying. Or so it seemed to me; I was burning up, sweat pouring off me. I could not get enough to drink. Someone remembered that saline injections strengthened contractions. As we had no syringe, they made me drink lukewarm salt water, which literally made me sick.

Someone else said there was a young refugee woman in the village who knew something about midwifery, having taken a course with the Red Cross. They actually found her and brought her to me. She appeared with a book under her arm: *Midwifery in Theory and Practice.* Unfortunately, her knowledge remained in the realm of theory; she had had no practical experience whatsoever. The woman read from her book. I heard phrases like "neck of the uterus . . . position of the child . . . dilatation and expulsion stages . . ." Ominously, everything seemed to come from the chapter on "Complications." When the contractions started up again after a brief respite, my nerves snapped, and I shouted, "For heaven's sake, get that woman out of here!"

Time passed, the day ended, night came again, but still no progress. "Our horsey just can't manage it." I felt myself getting weaker and weaker. When contractions came, I just let them wash over me, unable to assist as I should have by pushing or panting.

That night Mother, Frieda, and Fräulein Trautmann put their heads together, and Mother reached a decision: Glowitz had always had a regular midwife, and she might well still be there. She must be fetched, no matter what. Frieda agreed to go for her, with a hard salami as bait. She set off before dawn, and Fräulein Trautmann took her place by my bedside.

About three hours later, in broad daylight, Frieda returned in a rage, sausage still in hand. With characteristic bluntness, she reported, "The bitch doesn't have the guts." So there was a midwife, but she was afraid to come. Going from village to village was dangerous, and besides, it was forbidden. An exception could be made only if we got authorization from the Kommandatura, a written pass to show.

Mother looked at everyone, straightened up in spite of her exhaustion, and said, "I'll go and get the pass. Where is this Kommandatura?"

"Near the manor, in the house of Drambusch the forester."

"All right."

A small commotion ensued; in a panic, Father Jesko tried to dissuade Mother from going: "What if . . . what if they . . . Oh, you know what I mean!"

TO ZACKENZIN AND BACK

Mother did not wait to hear him out but set off at once. Now I, too, was seized with panic. As long as I had had Mother by my side, I had felt safe, for all the pain, the weakness, the fear. But after a nerve-racking hour Mother returned, paper in hand, and Frieda left for Glowitz at once.

Time dragged as we waited, and I got weaker and weaker. How long has it been? I wondered. With our watches gone, we had no way of knowing. Suddenly the midwife was there. She examined me and sighed: "Let's see if strong coffee helps. Do you have any?" Thanks be to God and to Marie's foresight, we did. It perked me up a little, enough to let me take in the following dramatic scene.

The midwife said, "She needs an injection, but I've only got one left, and that I'm saving for a friend of mine in Glowitz, who's due in a few days."

When Mother heard that, she took up a position in the doorway and said resolutely, "I won't stand for this. You can see it's a matter of life and death. You have a duty and an obligation to help those who need it most, irrespective of persons. You're not getting out of here until you give my daughter that injection."

The midwife opened her mouth to reply, thought better of it, and gave me the injection. Soon the contractions resumed. "Push now, push!"

A child is born. The fight for its entry into the world lasted thirty-seven hours or so, a night and a day, another night and part of another day, until three or four in the afternoon of March 23, 1945. I was utterly drained, probably closer to death than to life. It did not even register that the midwife had to stop me from hemorrhaging. Merely to open my eyes would have taken more strength than I had. But I could still hear, although everything sounded far away. Someone was saying, "Well, at least we saved the baby." And I heard my little girl crying.

A Spring Like No Other

Coffee Klatsch and Other Gatherings

Spring came early to Pomerania that year. Only the end of March, and already the air streaming through our open skylight was mild and balmy. Day after day the sun blazed in a cloudless sky.

Perhaps because of the fine weather, or because Mother's resoluteness had made a deep impression on her, quite on her own the midwife came over from Glowitz to look in on the baby and me. She weighed "her" product on a grain scale borrowed from Frau Musch. Not exactly a precision instrument, but she was pleased as punch with the result: "Four kilos–what a splendid specimen! No wonder it was such a hard birth, with the mother so delicate and the girl so big!"

The midwife's visit provided the occasion for afternoon coffee. Mother and Father Jesko, Frieda and Marie, Fräulein Trautmann, Fräulein Rahn, and Aunt Deten gathered around my bed. An important topic was broached: What name should the "splendid specimen" receive?

"Why, Claudia, of course," Mother said.

This name would never have occurred to me. "Why Claudia? Why of course?"

"To remind us of Klaus, your brother who was killed."

From Klaus to Claudia: quite a leap. But true to the pattern that had emerged in the last weeks, Mother got her way. I was lucky to be allowed to contribute the middle name Christina, for my youngest brother, Christian, of whom we had had no news at all. "And Emmy?" I added. That was my mother's given name, which she had always detested because as a child she was teased for having "a servant's name." But my request moved her, and she gave permission.

Now Frieda had something to say, but she hemmed and hawed. Finally she took a big swallow of coffee and with great embarrassment announced, "Baroness—I mean Mother—I'd like to change my state."

"What's this, Frieda? Have you gone mad? What in the world? At such a time—and who to?" The old Pomeranian expression "to change one's state" meant to get married.

"No, no, I didn't mean it like that—oh, dear me, no! But Anna, she's alone with the children, and she's so scared."

Anna was Frieda's sister, wife of the gardener on our estate in Rumbske, who, like most of our men, had been taken away by the war. The lodgings of the gardener and the chauffeur were in a cottage a bit outside the village, close to the manor. Emboldened by her walks to Glowitz, Frieda had crept out one evening to visit her sister. And now she wanted to move in with her and lend a hand. But she was terrified that the "lordships" would think their chambermaid was abandoning them.

"Nonsense, Frieda. That's a different matter altogether, and I think it's a very sensible decision. The time for chambermaids is past anyway. We'll have a little more space here, and one less mouth to feed can't hurt. Besides, what you've done for us over the last four days is something I'll never forget, never!" Whereupon Mother gave Frieda a big hug, which promptly transformed Frieda's relief back into embarrassment.

Frieda had more news to report, alas: our beautiful manor

house was no longer there. The Russians had burned it down, not right after their arrival, but a few days later. One night they had rolled drums of gasoline or alcohol into the house, dumped out the contents, and set fire to the place.

"They were celebrating outside on the carriage drive, and in the flower beds, dancing and singing. And drinking too—they were swilling it down; the distillery's got a lot stored up. And then they went and got women from the village, 'invited them up,' as they said. Anna and her children hid in the bushes by the icehouse, and she saw the whole thing. She said it was unbelievable, that's what she said."

A pause followed, during which we all pictured the scene. But curiosity is human nature, and we kept wondering why the Russians had burned the manor, when they could have used the place themselves and indeed been far more comfortable than anywhere in the village. Frieda reported the various explanations she had heard.

The first and most ridiculous version said that there had been looting, whether by Germans or Russians, whereupon the commandant, determined to impose order, had decided to eliminate the source of the problem.

Meanwhile we learned that the destruction of Warsaw was continuing, that the old cultural monuments were being blown up. There were four of these in particular for which we wept, whose destruction we felt as a personal loss: the Cathedral of Saint John in the old city, the Christ on the Cross in a suburb, intentionally shot down, and then, what I find particularly grotesque, the Brühl Palace, one of the most beautiful monuments of German architecture in Warsaw. The Nazis always said that Warsaw was a German city. So what possessed them to blow up the Brühl Palace? Senseless . . . And the Germans were astonished when the Russians burned down a couple of houses—when they themselves wantonly and brutally destroy the most priceless treasures of their own culture. And finally the Tomb of the Unknown Soldier was destroyed to its very foundations. Those aren't civilized human beings, we said, they are barbarians.[8]

The second version seemed to make a bit more sense: "In the hall, over the fireplace, there was that big painting of the late count, so handsome and colorful in his hussar's uniform—"

"As a captain of the Royal Hussars in Potsdam!" Father Jesko corrected her.

"Yes, Baron. Well, the Russians saw that painting and said, 'He must be the owner. He must be a really big wheel, a Party leader way high up, right behind that Hermann Göring. Not even a German general gets to wear a uniform like that. And a man like that has got to be punished.' "

But the likeliest explanation remained that the intoxication of victory and the thirst for revenge formed an explosive mixture. The slightest pretext, the smallest spark, must have been enough to ignite it.

Thinking of the Russians' drunken gathering, I suddenly recalled that I had been sharing my mattress with a bottle of champagne. Before we set out from home, I had opened a seam and stuffed the bottle into it, then sewed it up again. "Please get it out for me, Frieda. It's here near my head. Now or never is the time for a glass of champagne."

Father was dismayed: "Please, Libussa, this really isn't the time. . . ."

"Well, when on earth will it be? Should we wait till the Russians find it? I say this is the perfect time; we must drink to Frieda before she leaves, and to Claudia's arrival."

Our coffee cups and tin mugs did not exactly clink like champagne glasses, and of course the champagne was not chilled. But strange to say, the little mouthful each of us got did cheer us up.

"I Had to Concede"

A spring like no other. Carried by the columns of fugitives or victorious Russians, favored by the poor living conditions and perhaps also by the unseasonable warmth, epidemics spread like wildfire. Dysentery and typhoid and spotted fever were rife among the human beings, while the cows were plagued by hoof-and-mouth disease, the pigs by erysipelas, the horses by equinia.

Just a few days after giving birth, I came down with dysentery. The illness hit me doubly hard because I was already so weak. Lifting my hand or my head made me break out in a sweat, and I could not imagine getting up. One consequence was that I could no longer nurse my baby. Where to find milk—or steal it? This vexing question, a matter of life and death, would pursue me like a shadow from this time on.

As yet, there was no dire need. There were still plenty of cows, though no more deliveries to the dairy in Glowitz. In the short span between the collapse of German rule and the arrival of the Russians, feverish activity had filled the village: animals were slaughtered around the clock—calves, pigs, sheep, geese, and hens were sacrificed to people's fear of what the future might bring. Especially feverishly, salted and canned meat was hidden and buried. Some of this buried treasure fell to us. Our tenants in particular, but some independent farmers as well, looked after us, as though to demonstrate to their new overlords that they were keeping faith with the old "lordships." But secrecy had to be maintained; visitors came knocking only after dark or before daybreak, bearing gifts: a crock of honey, bread, milk. But how long could we continue this way?

As I lay there, without a shred of strength, disaster struck. Because a Russian was—allegedly—fired upon or shot, the commandant ordered the entire village evacuated, within an hour! Too weak to move, I was tied onto my mattress with ropes and maneuvered down the stairs to the ground floor. There an anxious wait began. An hour passed, a second hour, half a day. Then the evacuation order was rescinded, as abruptly as it had been issued.

Subsequent reports from Rumbske allowed us to figure out what had really been going on. There, too, they had received an order to evacuate—on account of some "partisan activity" that no German knew anything about. But this order was never rescinded. Men and women, old people and children, all had to leave the village and wait a long time until they received permission to return. They found that their houses had been ransacked and wrecked. It was a question of plunder, no more, no less.

In Rowen the Russians probably realized that there was no need to go to so much trouble. The looting raged day and night. No house, cellar, or attic was spared. They scoured barns and stables, pulled woodpiles apart, ran pitch forks through stacks of straw and hay and even through manure piles to see what might be hidden there. And they considered almost everything to be worth taking, from old-fashioned grandfather clocks to petticoats and brassieres. I sometimes tried to picture what this army might look like marching home someday, laden down with such spoils.

Hand in hand with the terrible went the bizarre. An order went forth, backed by the threat of dire punishment, as if it were a matter of lethal weapons: all "musical equipment" was to be surrendered—recorders, violins, trumpets, drums, accordions, pianos. The Russians took the hoard to the station at Neu-Klenzin, near Glowitz, where they simply left it piled up outdoors, exposed to the weather. Eventually, weeks later, children came across it and dragged home whatever still seemed usable.

The looters observed only one taboo, but that they observed religiously. No Russian soldier ever touched my laundry basket of baby things or even poked through it looking for adult contraband.

Along with the looting went rape. In that unprecedented spring, the victors were on the rampage. Women protected themselves as best they could. Faces streaked gray with ashes or dotted with red to suggest spotted fever, black kerchiefs tied low over their foreheads, they would hobble along like arthritic old crones. Sometimes it helped, usually it did not. But archangels must have been watching over the bed of the mother and her babe in arms. Lust subsided, the terrifying figures became human again. They patted the child and nodded and smiled at the mother. Then they would dig in their pockets to see if they hadn't some suitable gift, or, failing that, an unsuitable one: a lump of sugar, a pinch of tobacco.

"Yes, Russians adore children." I kept hearing people say that. But it was a description rather than an explanation. It was even harder, indeed almost impossible, to account for the second special role I came to play, not toward the perpetrators this time but toward their victims. A girl came to my bedside to have a good cry and be comforted. Others followed, and soon I had an almost unbroken stream of women seeking me out in my attic room. It began to irritate Mother and Father Jesko, because they had to vacate their room each time. Only when they were alone with me did the women feel uninhibited enough to speak. Besides, it generally took a long time for the sobbing and wailing to give way to coherent sentences. But once the words started flowing, they came pouring out. And in almost every case, the narrative began with the peculiar formula "I had to concede."

Where did this phrase come from? Who invented the euphemism, and how widespread was its use in the Russian-occupied territories? I could no more answer such questions than I could account for my popularity as mother-confessor-with-child. In any case, my role usually involved just crying with the battered and distraught woman, putting my arms around her, stroking her hair, and listening.

"I had to concede"—and strangely enough, keeping count seemed crucial: "Six times I had to concede." Sometimes I found it difficult to keep a straight face, for instance when a stocky woman already well along in years told me, "I had to concede twelve times—no, what am I saying, thirteen times I had to concede. My God, what do you say to that, Libussa?" Yes, what was there to say? Her horror seemed to contain a touch of pride at what she had endured.

But isn't it true that wherever the terrible occurs the grotesque and even the comic cannot be far behind? Tears and laughter are part of the human birthright. We feel at home in the rationality of everyday life, in our shell of normality. But when the rational fails, when the familiar is turned topsy-turvy, and sense becomes nonsense, we respond with tears—

or with laughter. And not infrequently one suddenly gives way to the other.

That explains why I started up in alarm when Father Jesko burst into the attic, shaking with helpless laughter. Something had happened, but what? It took Father several minutes to get it out, for each time he tried to speak he succumbed to fresh gales of laughter, which brought tears to his eyes. "Just now—no, it's unbelievable—just now Fräulein Trautmann had to concede!"

Father stopped in confusion only when he saw my own eyes fill with tears. I felt I owed the woman an apology. When the bony old maid had fled with the others to the moor to escape the Russians galloping up to the patriarch's farm, I had felt superior, wondering whether that was really necessary.

Marie's Heirloom

I remained confined to my mattress for four weeks. When I first attempted to get up and walk, I needed helping hands, for my head began to spin. But it was high time I assumed a vertical position again. No sooner was I halfway up and about than Mother came down with dysentery, and hoof-and-mouth disease too, which, though rarely dangerous to humans, was extremely painful. Ulcers formed in her mouth, making it impossible for her to eat.

It was also high time we looked for new accommodations. Even now, at the end of April, by afternoon our attic under the tarred roof became stifling, certainly only a foretaste of the hellish heat we could expect in the summer. Frau Musch was becoming unbearable too. We heard her carping all day long; she found something wrong with everybody and everything. She bickered with Mother and Marie, and began to bicker with me when I went down to the yard, looking for a tub in which to wash Claudia's diapers. The woman had an evil streak in her, envy of the gentry turned to vengefulness, something we encountered nowhere else.

But could new lodgings even be located? Our prospects seemed poor; the village still had twice its normal population. For that reason I felt tremendously excited when I heard of an apartment supposedly standing empty. I hurried to see it. Yes, the apartment existed, but in what a condition, and the stench! Had refugees or Russians been living there? Whoever they were, they obviously did not mind filth and saw no need to go all the way to the privy in the backyard. No wonder no one wanted to move in!

But we had no choice. I hurried back and told Marie. Then I made arrangements for our absence: Fräulein Rahn would do the cooking, Father Jesko and Fräulein Trautmann would look after Mother and the baby. Marie and I spent three days literally mucking the place out, scrubbing it clean. Not only the floors, but also the walls, the doors, and the windows all had to be washed several times. Three days, from morning till night, for a small two-bedroom apartment with a storeroom, kitchen, and hallway! At last it was ready for us to move into: Mother and Father Jesko, Marie, Claudia, and me. The Biedermanns, Fräulein Rahn, and Fräulein Trautmann would continue to sleep at Frau Musch's for the time being, spending the day with us.

Right away new difficulties appeared. We now had an apartment, but nothing to furnish it with. Our possessions consisted of my mattress, a kitchen knife and a teapot, a saucepan and a wooden spoon, three thermos bottles, and for each person a plate and a cup, a fork, a spoon, and a knife. We had a few extra cups. At night the parlor had to be converted to a dormitory, with straw on the floor.

We still had Hobble. A whole month's rest had brought no improvement in his condition. Either he had been born lame or he had been that way a long time. But for that very reason, the horse was invaluable. The Russians who looked him over lost interest the moment they saw his gait. Could we perhaps trade him for whatever we needed most urgently? That would be a kitchen table and benches to sit on; it was really tiring sitting on the floor all day, even for meals. So I set out to look, and soon came upon a farmer prepared to make the swap; he also agreed to provide a small can of milk for us every night.

I undertook more and more of these forays—stalking expeditions, Father called them—in search of usable items. Actually Father Jesko had no faith in my abilities, and he did not help matters with his constant nagging: "Libussa, don't go! The Russians will get you. Or shoot you. You're just asking for trouble."

True, I had to watch like a hawk. But between three and six in the morning our conquerors were wont to sleep the sleep of the just, and we all knew where their sentries were posted—in the courtyard of the manor, for instance. There was no need to run straight into their arms. So I simply closed my ears, or gave answers that upset Father even more: "Well, so what if they catch me—I doubt they'll kill me on the spot. If worse comes to worst, Mother can always bundle up Claudia and come to get me."

While making my rounds, I ran into the former chief inspector Hesselbarth. The old man could hardly keep back his tears when he saw me, and he did something he had never done before: he solemnly kissed my hand. When he heard of our plight, he said reproachfully, "But, Baroness Libussa, why didn't you come to see us? My wife and I would like to help. We have two spare beds up in the attic that no one's using . . ." What joy when I returned with the news! That same day the beds were brought over without incident, even though Herr Hesselbarth lived in the old manor in Rowen, surrounded by Russians, which explained why we had not called on him. We simply had not dared.

Others had displayed more courage than we had. Shortly after their arrival, the Russians had dragged the old man out of the manor into the village, planning to shoot him, perhaps to show the villagers they had been "liberated." But the village folk had gathered, the women in the lead and with them the French POWs, and shouted that Herr Hesselbarth wasn't the "lord," he was their father. They crowded around him, their bodies forming a wall. Their loyalty, which saved his life, was Herr Hesselbarth's reward for the many years during which he had carried out his duties with utmost fairness and kindliness.

My next encounter proved less gratifying, and far from harmless. A man suddenly leapt out of the bushes as I passed. His face was blackened, and from the bulge in his cape I surmised that he had a gun. Not a Russian, but our forester, Drambusch. He had been the most fanatical Nazi for miles around, and obviously he had not given up yet. He had built himself a "bunker" somewhere in the forest or on the moors. Now he insisted that I take him to Father Jesko.

"No! Why should I?"

Drambusch refused to be dissuaded. His eyes glowed wildly, he seized my arm and pushed me forward. Apparently he intended to continue the struggle as a "werewolf." "Side by side with the baron, for Führer and Fatherland, until the Courland Army comes to our rescue! I have another carbine and plenty of ammunition."

Father Jesko, awakened in the middle of the night, flew into a rage. "Are you out of your mind, man? Do you want your family to pay for this? Or mine? Or the whole village?"

"But, Baron, Major . . ."

Father took the forester, who looked puny next to him, by the scruff of the neck and gave him a good shaking. "I want you out of here this minute, or I'll take you to the Kommandatura myself!" The werewolf slunk off and was never seen again. Later we heard that the Russians had hunted him down and shot at him as he tried to run away. Wounded, he was taken to Stolp, where he died in misery.

The incident alarmed me, but not for long. A notion popped into my head and soon became a plan: why not extend my stalking expeditions as far as Rumbske? I might find something useful in the manor, ruin though it was. The park and the overgrown ravine between the gardener's cottage and the manor would provide cover until I was practically at the doorstep.

But a plan is one thing and executing it another. I was unprepared for the sight of the stumps of chimneys, the blackened remnants of wall, the steps that once led up to the veranda, now ending in space. These were not just any old ruins—they were the ruins of my childhood and youth. I could not bring myself to poke around like a looter; I turned back. But on the way home, my anger won out, and I thought: You foolish girl; you can't afford to be sentimental now. Today was a waste of time, but tomorrow you're going to try again!

And I did. I discovered that although the first and second floors were a wasteland, with rubble and charred beams wherever I looked, the side entrance to the cellar still existed; I had only to clear away the stones that blocked it, and then I could squeeze through. I followed the passage that led to the kitchen. The rooms on the left had caved in, and everything had been cleared out of the rooms on the right. That was the estate office, where Herr Rodemerk once reigned. Here Frieda had lived, there Marie. On to the kitchen. I found two saucepans, a frying pan, a ladle, and the iron coffee roaster. What treasures!

And now the coachmen's sitting room, with Uncle Biedermann's murals. Two fine chairs brought down from the hall upstairs: handsome Empire chairs. And the heavy oak table from the library, which we had used for Aunt Deten's séance only a few weeks before, or was it an eternity? Shards of crystal on the table and the floor. I gathered them up, sat down and examined them. What were they from? Wasn't this a bit of gold from a rim? And a piece of a carved hunting scene? The Fortune of Edenhall . . . The verses of the poem passed through my mind: how prophetic they were, telling of changed fortunes and the smashing of the goblet that had symbolized those fortunes.

With the kitchen utensils, I made my way back to Rowen. The following night I borrowed a wheelbarrow to transport the chairs. Then a problem arose: I could no possible move the table by myself, and nothing would induce Father Jesko to go with me. The Kommandatura had imposed a curfew from eight in the evening to six in the morning, and orders were orders. So I took Marie aside and painted a glowing picture of how wonderful it would be to have the table, and how well it would go with the chairs. But Marie was terrified.

Finally I said, "Think how valuable that table is now. And tomorrow, or the next day, it'll be even more valuable. You couldn't get a piece of furniture like that anymore."

That made an impression. Finally her practicality won out over any worries she might have had. "Well, all right, I'll go with you . . . but on one condition . . . don't be cross with me, Libussa. I just wanted . . ."

"Go on, tell me!"

"Well, I'll only go with you if you promise I can inherit it one day."

It was evident that this was not acquisitiveness on her part, just something to help her over her fear, a kind of crutch. With Mother as witness, I solemnly promised what the moment demanded. Then we set out. It took every last bit of our strength to lift the table, drag it up out of the ruined manor, and haul it back to Rowen. From that time on, we always referred to it as Marie's heirloom.

A Peculiar Peace

An exalted word was in the air: *kultura.* To be sure, it hardly took on the aura the conquerors had in mind. *"Russki kultura"* did indeed enter our language, but people who used it would grimace, to suggest that they found the prevailing conditions revolting.

Kultura was supposed to manifest itself first of all in cleanliness and order, with insistence on two measures: the main street of the village had to be swept daily, and whenever a new commandant arrived, it had to be strewn with white sand and adorned with fir trees on either side. Since these saplings dried out as quickly as the commandants changed, replanting the ceremonial avenues became an almost constant undertaking.

Next, *kultura* was to make itself felt in the pigsties and

cowsheds. Pigs had to be scrubbed till they gleamed, likewise the cows and horses. Not a speck of dust or a wisp of straw was allowed to sully their coat. For currying, men were needed, and Father Jesko was pressed into service. Sometimes he came home with a piece of bread for his pains, or a few potatoes—but chiefly he came home with lice. We were duly alarmed; didn't lice carry spotted fever? We were not sure whether that applied to horse lice, but in our fear of contagion we waged a bitter and largely ineffectual battle against the pests.

One day word came that every house had to be decked out in festive green, as at Whitsun. The Russians paraded through the village, firing shots into the air, waving to us, and shouting, *"Woina kaputt! Woina kaputt!"* What had happened? Was the war really over? Would peace come now? And in what form?

We had no idea. Our world had shrunk to our own village and its immediate environs. We saw no newspapers, and all wireless sets had had to be turned in. Even if someone had kept one hidden away, there would have been no electric power to run it. Either the generating plants were no longer operating, or the lines had been destroyed.

As of midnight, the guns have fallen silent on all fronts. On orders from the Supreme Admiral of the Fleet, the Wehrmacht has ceased the struggle, which has become hopeless. With that, almost six years of heroic struggle are at an end. It has brought us great victories and grave defeats. In the end, the German Wehrmacht honorably succumbed to forces vastly superior in number.

True to his oath, the German soldier has given his utmost for his people, achieving unforgettable deeds. To the very end, our homeland supported him with all its might, sustaining heavy sacrifices. The unparalleled achievement of both military and civilian population will receive its definitive recognition when the just verdict of history is handed down at some later date.

Even the enemy cannot fail to respect the achievements and sacrifices of the German soldier on land, on sea, and in the air. Every soldier can therefore lay down his arms with pride and dignity and, in these gravest hours of our history, bravely and confidently go to work to assure that our people may live forever.

In this grave hour, the Wehrmacht remembers its fallen comrades. The dead enjoin us to manifest unconditional loyalty, obedience, and discipline toward our Fatherland, bleeding now from countless wounds.[9]

If the war was now indeed over, and peace on the march, the signs announcing it were rather peculiar. With the exception of some small farm implements, all agricultural machinery was registered, assembled out in the fields on the edge of the villages, and hauled away. Plows and harrows, drilling and threshing machines, harvesters and tractors, all disappeared. Even Max and Moritz, the venerable steam-plow locomobiles that Grandfather had bought around the turn of the century, gave a farewell toot and tumbled off down the road, slowly but surely. What would happen now; how would people sow and harvest? And how could the vanquished survive in this new peace if the fields lay fallow?

On the heels, so to speak, of our agricultural machinery followed our public transportation, the local branch line of the railroad. The rails were to be dismantled. To be exact, the dismantling had already begun at the end of the line, in Dargeröse, and was working its way toward the provincial capital, Stolp. Now the stretch between Rowen and Rumbske had been reached, and the younger women from both villages had to report to work, Marie and I included.

It was heavy work, work to which women had probably never been assigned before, at least not in this country. The rails had to be loosened, with enormous wrenches, from the crossties to which they were bolted—and rusted. Then they had to be hoisted up, carried, and heaved onto the waiting flatbeds. Then the flatbeds had to be pushed along so that work on the next segment of track could begin. The demolition proceeded slowly from our station to the Wossek

Woods, then past the station at Bandsechow, and on to Gutzmerow. The work continued from morning till night, day after day. We got a break only at midday, when we were given barley or potato soup, sometimes with a suggestion of meat in it. Not until we reached Gutzmerow were we replaced by women from the next villages and permitted to go home, heaving a sigh of relief.

I used the opportunity to visit our friends in Gutzmerow. Frau von Hanstein and her sister were living in a small house right on the main road, which left them especially vulnerable to the waves of victors sweeping up and down that road. They had a terrible story to tell. The sisters' father was a celebrated surgeon, head physician at the hospital in Stolp, and known—respectfully—by young and old as the "Pomeranian butcher." Before the Russians arrived, the parents fled to Gutzmerow, planning to join their daughters and continue on from there with two wagons. The two sisters sat in one wagon, Frau von Hanstein's children with the grandparents in the other. In the chaos and confusion that ensued when the refugees encountered a column of tanks, the family became separated. The doctor had cyanide tablets with him. He gave them to his grandchildren and his wife, and took some himself. The sisters survived.

How *could* one survive something like that? The answer was simple. Frau von Hanstein's sister had been pregnant. By now the child had been born, a healthy boy, two weeks old. The sisters told me that if they had been alone, they would certainly have put an end to it. But the child kept them going, made it all worthwhile. . . . No need for them to ask me whether I understood; as we said goodbye, we promised to see each other as often as we could.

No sooner was the work on the railroad over than the next consequence of peace became manifest: in the meadows near Rowen, the Russians gathered a huge herd of cattle, all the animals from the estates of Rowen, Rumbske, and perhaps others. The farmers and tenant farmers also lost their calves and cows. Only a few animals were spared. The occupying force kept some for its own needs, while others—just a handful—had been hidden in time, for instance in the "Swedish fortifications," which were doing their duty again after three hundred years.

Now the Russians wanted the herd driven somewhere, and again they recruited women. Again I was among the chosen. A long march now commenced, "to the east," as they told us—that could mean anything. With Russians on horseback circling constantly around us, the cattle and the women moved past Wedding Hill to the main road, where we headed in the direction of Lauenburg. Our chief task was milking; the full udders had to be relieved morning and night. Milk, milk, literally overflowing, and all just squirted onto the ground, into the grass from which it had come. I kept thinking of the children, of my baby. How would I feed her from now on? The farmer to whom I had traded Hobble had been giving me milk, but now he, too, had lost his cows.

The first night, then the second. We stopped in the Leba Valley, beyond Zezenow. The herd was left to graze down by the river, while we spent the night in a barn. Whispered discussions: "Now's the time to make a dash for it," I said. "The farther we get from home, the harder it'll be."

"No, no. They'll notice right away. They'll catch us, arrest us, and drag us off God knows where."

"Who can be sure? Probably they'll just round up replacements in the next village."

"No, no . . ." Nothing I could say made any difference; all these women were terrified, unwilling to take any chances. So I crept out alone, checked the sentries, dozing not too far off, and headed for home. Was I braver than the others? Hardly. Again, a greater fear motivated me, my fear for my child. That explained why I set off at a gallop, with complete disregard for all possible dangers, and arrived back in Rowen before dawn.

The baby was crying with hunger, crying and crying. A mash of cooked nettles and dandelion, a gruel cooked with water—such things could serve as a supplement in a pinch, but they did not provide the basic nourishment a tiny creature barely two months old needed. Because I could not show myself in the village so soon, Mother and Marie sallied forth in search of milk, with little packets of coffee beans to barter with. The yield was meager. A quarter liter here, a cup of goat's milk there: it helped for the moment, but was simply not enough.

Soon, in addition to hunger, the baby was suffering from chronic diarrhea. Nothing seemed to do any good, not even the decoction we obtained from an old herbalist, whom we sought out in desperation. Now Claudia hardly cried anymore; she was becoming weaker and weaker.

Finally Marie had an inspiration. "The distiller's wife in Rumbske, Magdalena Vietzke, she's forever having babies—all girls too! She's just had another one, the fifth—no, the sixth. Remember how our old Vietzke was always bragging about his daughter-in-law's milk supply, how it would break records, how she could feed a dozen? Well, I was wondering. Do you suppose it's the same this time?"

"Our old Vietzke" was our former butler; his son was the village distiller. I promptly wrapped the baby in a blanket and set off with her. The Kommandatura had taken up quarters in the distillery with the Vietzkes, but that could not be helped. As it happened, I encountered no difficulties; no one barred my way.

"Oh, Frau Libussa, the poor little thing, she looks all peaked. . . . Of course I've got milk enough for two—just give her to me!" Frau Vietzke put the baby to her breast, and Claudia drank and drank, until she fell blissfully asleep.

From now on, I walked to Rumbske three times a day with the little bundle in my arms, which protected me against unwelcome advances. Within a week the baby was blooming, as though she had never been in danger of starving.

The Soldier and the Grandmother

They say happiness makes you forget anything but the present; happiness is complete immediacy, the fulfilled moment, which begins to melt away as soon as you beg it to tarry.

Odd, though: if happiness were only that and nothing more, it would be indistinguishable in its effects from unhappiness, from terror. Where terror reigns, one's horizons close in mercilessly. One cares only about what is happening in the present moment and has to react instantaneously, without hesitation; survival depends on it.

Gradually, almost imperceptibly, a change made itself felt. Perhaps habit had toughened us, perhaps new hopes were secretly welling up inside us. Very cautiously we lifted our heads, put out feelers, looked about, and our horizons widened a little. We began to wonder, for instance, how others—friends and neighbors—had fared.

We heard one piece of good news: the old Glowitzers, Great-Uncle Gerhard and Great-Aunt Lena, had come through unscathed, even though they had not left their house. As in the case of Chief Inspector Hesselbarth, a few courageous souls came to their defense, people who had worked on their estate and the French POWs again.

But then we received more and more grim tidings. Many people had actually carried out what we had planned to do: they escaped the brutality of the conquerors by shooting or hanging themselves. Others took poison, like the surgeon from Stolp—and many other doctors. Many, indeed more than many, people were murdered, and many were taken away, never to be seen again. Sometimes we could hardly believe our ears: An elderly couple were chased into the village pond and forced to stay there until they drowned in the icy water. A man was hitched to a plow and driven until he keeled over, when a burst from a submachine gun finished him off. The proprietor of the Grumbkow estate, Herr von

Livonius, had his arms and legs hacked off and was thrown, still alive, to the pigs.

Mother's uneasiness was growing; we had had no news at all from Karzin, barely twenty kilometers away, so we did not know what had happened to my grandmother, Frau Liebe. I decided to go and find out. I had never walked this particular stretch, but I had driven it many times. Starting with the Wossek near Rumbske, forests would provide cover for most of the way; it would be possible to avoid the villages altogether.

Mother accepted my plan at once, but Father Jesko objected, as always. In fact, he bitterly opposed my scheme: "Libussa, it won't work; you mustn't even try."

"And why not, if I may ask?"

"Well, it's too far—not as the crow flies, but the actual route, which is at least one third longer. And then you won't be walking on roads, but cross-country. You won't make it."

"That's silly. I'm in excellent condition—I'm out walking every day, often for long distances over all sorts of terrain."

"That's bad enough. I keep warning you, but you won't listen. And besides, you're bound to get lost; you don't have a map or a compass."

"Am I an idiot? Am I one of your soldiers?" I was losing my temper.

"Libussa!"

"No, really, this is ridiculous. I know where I'm going, I know the way, and I can always follow the railroad bed if need be."

Father had run out of arguments, so he started to shout: "I don't want you going! I won't let you!"

Strange: while he was shouting, I suddenly noticed his hands. They were moving about constantly, the fingers drumming on the table—no, they were trembling. I realized that he felt unsure of himself. Or perhaps, though he would never have admitted it, he was afraid. More and more I had been taking the initiative, doing what circumstances required. All this had left Father Jesko disoriented and discouraged; his image of the world and his sense of himself had crumbled.

Suddenly I felt how unfair I was being. Father was afraid not for himself but for Mother and me. What he had lost was his pride, his male role as our protector.

My anger melted away, and as gently as I could, I said, "Sorry, Father, but it won't do any good to forbid me. I'm going to Karzin, and I'll be back in no time." The next morning I set off before daybreak.

This spring of 1945 had continued as sunny and warm as it had begun. One could almost feel summer in the offing. True, deer no longer browsed by the road; mounted or motorized killers had ruthlessly mowed them down. But in the woods, away from the roads taken by the armies, I did come across deer, and wild boar too—a sow with her young. Also rabbits and a fox. All around me woodpeckers were hammering, cuckoos calling, wood pigeons cooing. I even heard an oriole. At the same time, I had to keep my eyes and ears open for the enemy. But I did not meet any Germans or Russians, and I reached Karzin before the noonday heat set in.

"Frau von Puttkamer, our lady? Oh, she lives in the castle, where else?" The woman working in her garden at the edge of the village put her hands on her hips indignantly, as though my cautious question were absolutely superfluous.

"Really? Upstairs, as before?"

"Well, upstairs is the cellar now. And the Kommandatura is sort of in the house too." She glanced suspiciously at me. "Tell me, miss, what would you be wanting of our lady?"

"I just want to visit her—I'm her granddaughter from Rumbske."

"Ah! Well, then!" The woman put her hoe aside, giving the weeds in the lettuce patch a short reprieve, and escorted me by a path that ran along the backs of all the gardens almost to my destination. We stopped and peeked out from a clump of bushes. "All clear! Give her my regards, won't you now!" I dashed over to the cellar door and slipped inside.

"Libussa, my dear, dear child!" The old woman, now in her eighty-third year, jumped up and threw her arms around me. Ah, my grandmother: still as agile and graceful as always, "my little mountain goat," as she was sometimes called by my grandfather, who had died four years earlier. But her most striking quality was her big and loving heart, hence her nickname of Frau Liebe. Also, she was funny and quick-witted, and could make up delightful comic rhymes on the spur of the moment. But when necessary, she proved her courage and mettle—I often thought she had steel in her spine.

Grandmother had two women sharing her cellar apartment: her sister Miriam and her faithful housekeeper, confidante, and friend, Hannah Brandt. For a while I had no chance to ask them any questions, because I had to give a full report on our experiences. Fortunately, they had a strictly observed routine: after lunch, which consisted of nettle soup, boiled potatoes, and dandelion salad, Frau Liebe asked for a break; she wished to "withdraw," as they always called it, and she and Aunt Miriam went into the next room for their afternoon nap. That gave Hannah Brandt an opportunity to tell me a dramatic story.

The first act took place in Lübzow, two kilometers from Karzin, on the way to Stolp. Eberhard von Braunschweig, an implacable opponent of the Nazis, lived there. He had been repeatedly warned and interrogated, even banished from Pomerania for a while, and arrested several times, most recently after the failed attempt on Hitler's life of July 20, 1944. When the Russians came, he stayed at home; after all, what did he, known far and wide as an anti-Nazi, have to fear from them? But the conquerors, drunk with victory and other things as well, saw in him only the landed aristocrat, not the anti-Fascist. They gave him no chance to explain: Eberhard von Braunschweig and his family were dragged out of their house and shot.

In Karzin, people knew the Russians were coming. From Lübzow sounds of shooting, the roar of tank engines, and the clattering of tank treads could be heard clearly as night fell. But Frau Liebe decided it was time for bed and "withdrew." A few minutes later, soldiers came storming into the house. One of them, submachine gun at the ready and still smoking, so to speak, appeared in Grandmother's bedroom.

Outside the church in Glowitz, 1944.
The groom is wearing the regulation steel helmet.

The wedding party. From the far right: Father Jesko, Mother, and Grandmother, known as Frau Liebe. Also on the right, third from top, wearing glasses, Great-Uncle Gerhard, the "old Glowitzer." His granddaughter

Otti von Veltheim, later to accompany Libussa on her hazardous journey from the West back to Pomerania, stands just behind the left shoulder of the bridegroom, Jobst von Oldershausen.

Memories of an untroubled childhood—Libussa with her mother and the two brother

Klaus-Wilhelm and Hans-Kaspar, who fell as young lieutenants early in the war.

Father Jesko in a photograph from the 1930s.

"Take good care of the babushka in the cellar"
—Frau Liebe, the grandmother from Karzin.

“There goes Prussia”—Mother.

Libussa and her daughter Claudia, shortly after arriving in the West.

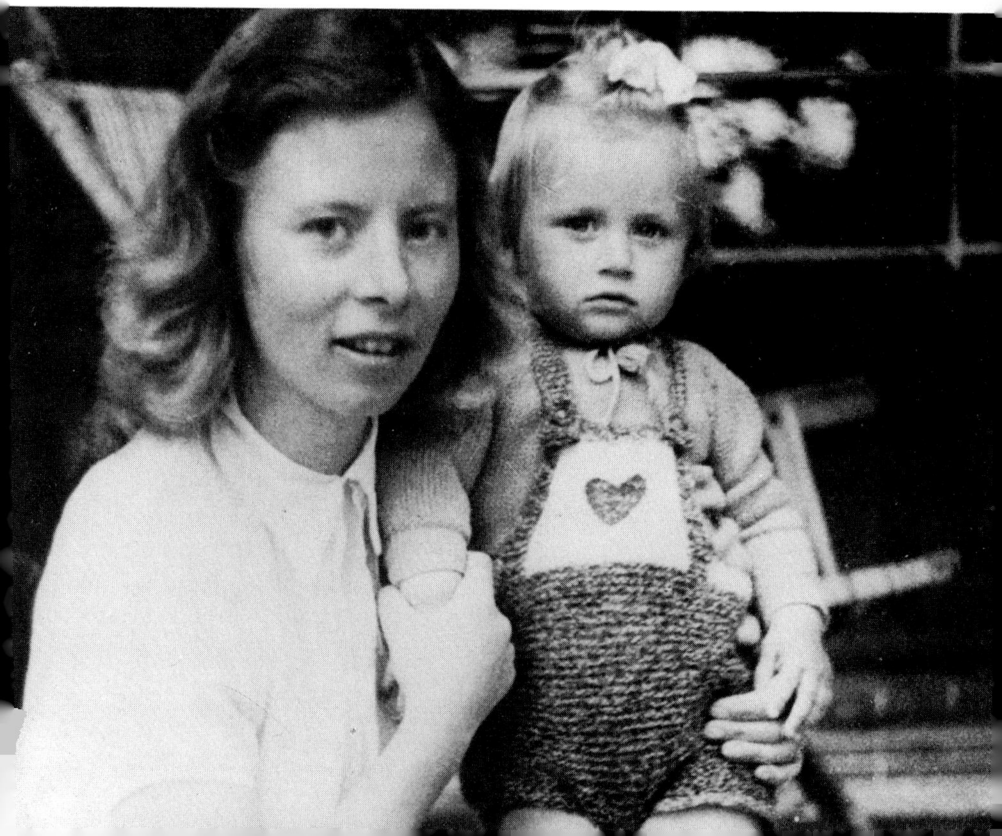

Four generations of women,
in a photograph taken around 1950.

He indicated what he had been up to in the next village and demanded that she vacate her bed, so he could sleep it off. But Frau Liebe told him it could not be done; this was her bed, she was an old woman, and she needed her sleep. But he could stretch out on the bedside rug, and she could let him have a blanket and a pillow. "I can pray for us both," she said, and folded her hands and said the Lord's Prayer. The bloodthirsty warrior, baffled, dumbfounded, and impressed, did as he was told. And so the soldier and the grandmother spent the rest of the night peacefully side by side.

"Oh, Libussa," Hannah said in conclusion, "it was a ghastly night. I'll never forget it. We women, you know . . . But in the morning I pulled myself together and crept into the bedroom. Just imagine! Here I am braced for the worst, and instead I find this idyllic scene, the soldier and your grandmother. Coming in, I woke them both. 'Good morning,' said Frau Liebe. And the soldier quietly pulled on his boots, put his cap on, straightened his tunic, and slung his submachine gun over his shoulder. Then he saluted and marched off."

"Hannah, what a miraculous story! But supposing peace ever comes: who will believe it?"

"Well, it's true. Look, this is the rug. We call it the 'Russian cot' now, and anyone who comes for the night sleeps on it. You can try it out for yourself tonight—it's all we have."

"Tell me what happened after that."

"Well, it went on in pretty much the way it began. Of course we had to move down here, with just these two rooms, the one Frau Liebe and Miriam occupy, and this one, with my bed in it and this table. But we manage, and having the Kommandatura upstairs even has its advantages. We're not assaulted or looted in here. And if the commandant wants his office nice and warm, the central heating warms our rooms too; sometimes we even get a bit to eat from them. But Frau Liebe's the key to it all. She's our shield, because the Russians are in awe of her, even the commandants."

"But don't they keep changing, as they do in Rowen?"

"Of course they do. But it makes no difference; the tradition just gets handed down from one to the next. Sometimes I think there must be some official piece of paper, an order that says, 'Watch over the babushka in the cellar, and watch yourself: don't take any liberties with her!' Or perhaps it's simply because Frau Liebe always deals with these men in such a friendly and dignified way, completely fearless and natural. And forceful, too, when she has to be. Recently she asked a young Russian if he didn't know who she was. 'But of course,' he said. 'Why?' Because he hadn't returned her greeting. The man was clearly shaken, and I think if the commandant had got wind of it, the soldier would have been in trouble. Anyway, since then she's always greeted properly."

"I think I'm beginning to understand what the woman in the village meant when she said, 'Upstairs is the cellar now. And the Kommandatura is sort of in the house too.' "

"Well, I'm afraid that's an exaggeration. But Frau Liebe still goes and visits the sick in the village, even though she can't bring them anything now. Although actually she brings them the most important thing of all—comfort and encouragement. It can't hurt that the Russians hear good things about her in the village."

When Frau Liebe and Aunt Miriam finished their after-lunch naps, we continued exchanging stories, and the afternoon and evening passed in a flash. Then I stretched out on the "Russian cot" and fell asleep at once.

As the sky began to grow light, I set off for home, sped on my way by the good tidings I was bearing. In the first rays of the sun, pearls of dew glittered in the grass, every breath of air was perfumed, the birds struck up their morning chorus. It really was a spring like no other. . . .

Summer in the Gardener's Cottage

The Call of the Screech Owl

The Government General project is the most unique creation of the NSDAP. It must be our goal to conquer this land entirely for the German Volk spirit. This will certainly have been achieved within a few decades, perhaps sooner. It will unquestionably be the case, as the Führer observed recently over dinner, that the Governor General's objective will be to make the Government General the most Aryan province in the whole German Reich. My reply to the Führer was: I take you at your word, Sir, and that is precisely our intention; because of the Jews we have sunk very low; without them let us rise to new heights. The Führer has promised me that in the foreseeable future the Government General will be entirely freed of Jews. In addition, a clear decision has been made that the Government General is to be German living space. Where today twelve million Poles live will one day be four to five million Germans. The Government General must become as German as the Rhineland. And if anyone should say to me: That's impossible—well, I can only reply: Did it seem any more likely we would now be in Cracow and have Party centers in Warsaw and Lublin than that this country, which we already control, should become German?[10]

Frieda came to Rowen to say goodbye again, this time for good. With her sister Anna and Anna's two children, she wanted to leave Rumbske and go to stay with relatives. "And then perhaps on to Germany, into the Reich."

"To Germany, into the Reich? What's that supposed to mean; where do you think we are now?"

Frieda was not too sure. "Well, it's just that you hear all these rumors."

But our main topic of conversation was the gardener's quarters in Rumbske that would now become available; Frieda wondered whether we would be interested in moving in. A great deal–indeed, almost everything–spoke in favor of it. Rumbske was our real home; and the place there had more room than our present accommodations. It bordered directly on our old park, where we could gather firewood, and on the manor's large garden, with a profusion of fruit and vegetables. The kitchen had running water, which would mean we would not have to haul it from a pump in the yard, as we did now. And last but not least: the distillery where the milk for Claudia flowed was only a hop, skip, and jump away.

The move was almost a fait accompli, when Father Jesko brought out his reservations: what would the Russians say when they heard the "lordships" had come home?

It was perfectly possible they would say nothing at all. We had been living for weeks now in Rowen, only two kilometers from Rumbske, unmolested, or at least no more molested than the other inhabitants. They must have known who we were. So why these constant anxieties? I felt myself getting angry, and I said, "Well, we can find out. Tomorrow morning, when I take Claudia to the distillery, I'll call on the commandant and ask for permission."

That I should not have said. Reproaches came raining down on me: my recklessness, my lack of responsibility, my behavior in general. But this scene settled it for me. The next day I paid my call, with the baby in my arms and master distiller Walter Vietzke at my side; in his daily dealings with the Russians he had picked up some scraps of their language. The conversation proved difficult; we had to rely more on gestures than on words, and in the end we were confronted with a surprise: The commandant said he had no authority to decide; I should apply to the Polish mayor.

The Polish mayor? That was the first mention I had heard of such a person. Or had I, had all of us, in our preoccupation with the Russians, failed to notice a second occupying force coming in? As I walked through the village to call on this other office, I began to make sense of things I had been seeing and hearing lately but failed to take in. Yes, more and more Poles had been turning up, in addition to those here before as POWs or forced laborers. They were taking over one farm after another; masters and servants were exchanging roles. And hadn't someone said recently that he had come across the "milice," a special combination of militia and police, distinguished from the Russians by the cut of their cap? We had also heard that all the shops in Glowitz were in Polish hands now, and you had to pay in zlotys, not in reichsmarks or rubles.

The mayor had taken over his German predecessor's office, on August Kuschel's farm. He sat behind a desk covered with papers. While I explained what had brought me there, he looked at me searchingly. I gave all of our names, and a smile flitted across his face when he heard Father Jesko's. Then the official finger glided down a page, was licked, turned the leaf, more pages—obviously a list of inhabitants. Finally it tapped on one entry: "The gardener's cottage, previously inhabited by Rudolf and Anna Kaminsky, née Sonnemann?"

"Yes."

"No objections; very good." Again the fixed smile, and a gesture: Dismissed; next, please—although no one was waiting outside. Deep down, my relief at having secured a sort of official approval was mixed with uneasiness. Might this "very good" mean: I'll have you under my control?

Whatever the case, our move was quickly effected. We borrowed Hobble back from the farmer, and he pulled our cartload of belongings to Rumbske. He was as lame as ever, but tough and willing.

Grete Krupps, who occupied the other half of the cottage,

gave us a warm welcome and helped us move in. Not only had Anna and Frieda left the place spotless; they had also left us real treasures to make our lives more comfortable: chairs, for instance, to complete the seating around Marie's heirloom; even curtains in the windows. Other problems also found solutions: Fräulein Rahn had already moved in with Berta and Grandma Kreft, and we managed to locate a bedroom in the village for the Biedermanns, complete with bed. Fräulein Trautmann came to the brave decision to venture forth into the unknown, in hopes of making her way back to her home in faraway Wuppertal.

These almost comfortably equipped lodgings, with their quiet setting under the ancient trees of the manorial park, seemed perfect for a summer idyll. But the idyll soon showed its dark side: precisely because of its isolated setting, the gardener's cottage offered a ready target for marauders. In the village this sort of thing had died down, and we even heard that a strict ban on looting had been issued to maintain or restore discipline among the troops.

To my great consternation, I have established that in defiance of the orders we have issued, looting takes place, sometimes of the most dreadful kind, such as armed robbery of the local populace or stealing a family's only cow, as well as roving about and burglarizing houses in the absence of the occupants. Other base crimes, such as dreadful rapes, likewise occur, especially in areas behind the lines. These shameful deeds betoken to an alarming degree a weakening of discipline, especially among units not engaged in combat. It is high time that we terminated these unauthorized forms of provisioning, these robbing sprees, long-distance looting excursions, indeed all pointless criminal activity.[11]

But where no one can see what is happening, no amount of orders will make any difference. Bandits stormed into the house at night, occasionally wearing masks. We did not bother to lock the door, because it would only have been broken down. The less the robbers found to make their raids worthwhile, the more havoc they wreaked. It took us hours to render the devastated place habitable again.

Only one circumstance afforded us at least occasional relief: Grete Krupps had a Russian corporal as her lover. And what was wrong with that? She had not seen her husband for years, had not heard from him in months. He that is without sin, let him first cast a stone. The benefit for us was that on those evenings when the corporal, who was stationed in a nearby village, clattered up on his horse and hitched it to the bench in front of the house, we knew we would have an undisturbed night.

Another and worsening problem was food. Claudia was still loyally provided for by her wet nurse, and a new and energetic commandant had managed to assemble a modest herd in the Rumbske cowsheds. Since then the youngest children got an allowance of half a liter of milk a day. But everywhere one felt the impact of the loss of the farm machinery and the livestock. People worried about the future: hardly anyone was willing to give up supplies he had managed to hoard. Potatoes could still be had, but already flour was in short supply. We stretched ours with ground-up birch bark, and Walter Vietzke let us have liquid yeast from the distillery for our baking. The bread we made tasted like the real thing, but it had the unfortunate characteristic of going moldy almost at once, especially now, in the summer heat. By the third morning, sometimes even by the second, we had to cut away the green patches, and by the fourth day hardly any edible portions remained. Fats and eggs were unobtainable, and we had meat only because of Marie's foresight. She guarded her barrel of salted meal with her life. On Sundays each of us received a tiny helping, and any bones were boiled three times for stock.

The worse the shortages, the more tempting the garden at the old manor became. It had beds of rhubarb, spinach, and lettuce, also raspberry, gooseberry, and currant bushes. Peas we had had planted before we set out on our trek would be ready to pick, and the early apples seemed more plentiful than ever before.

SUMMER IN THE GARDENER'S COTTAGE

Unfortunately, though, the Russians had taken over the garden and posted a sentry there around the clock. But he deterred us as little as Father Jesko's feeble objections. The garden was large, the sentry could not be in two places at once, and in the stillness of the night his boots could be heard crunching up and down the gravel paths. In the long wall separating the garden from the park, we found a hole, which I gradually enlarged until it was perfect for slipping into and out of the garden.

While I, equipped with a basket, set out on my raid, Mother would stand guard. She had relearned and rehearsed to perfection a skill she possessed as a girl: opening and closing her hands over her mouth and hooting to mimic the call of the screech owl. Three calls meant: careful, something suspicious. And two calls with a short interval between them meant: red alert. That call of the screech owl, once so familiar, now so rarely heard. But years later, whenever I heard one, I felt myself transported back to the garden at Rumbske, where I would crouch under the raspberries, listening for danger.

Scouting Party and Spinach

Frieda's curious remark about Germany and the Reich, Fräulein Trautmann's departure for Wuppertal, the invasion of the Poles, bringing their own mayor, their "milice," and their zlotys: all these seemed to be fragments of a puzzle, but as yet no picture emerged. My mind kept circling uneasily around the question: Where will all this lead?

If the war was really over and Pomerania was being transformed into a kind of inverted Government General, with the Poles as masters and the Germans as slaves, it made little sense to stay and wait while the food supplies ran out and winter closed in, perhaps bringing death by starvation. Better to try to make for the west, whatever the risk, if any opening could be found. Somewhere over there, west of the Oder, or perhaps even of the Elbe, there had to be territories occupied not by the Poles and the Russians but by the Americans and the British. The last Wehrmacht report we had heard said they had reached the Rhine, and they would not have stopped there. I thought of my friend M., who had married into an estate in Holstein a few years earlier; might we find a refuge there?

Unfortunately, no one had any accurate information. We were awash in rumors, alternately frightening and hopeful. How could we make plans under such circumstances? Should we leave our gardener's cottage on the strength of vague hopes, abandon our few hard-won possessions, only to end up stranded somewhere? That would be disastrous, and for the baby it might mean death. We could not risk simply setting out like Fräulein Trautmann.

But in Stolp there were probably army headquarters, perhaps even civilian authorities, who had an overview of the situation. Stolp also had a railroad station, from which long-distance trains had once departed. Were they still running, or running again, and would they take Germans wishing to emigrate? These possibilities had to be investigated.

I drew Mother aside to discuss my plan with her first. I would need three days: one to walk to Karzin, one to reach Stolp and make my inquiries, and one to return to Rumbske. Straightforward as ever, Mother said, "Yes, child, that's a sensible idea. I say try it!" Together we approached Father Jesko; I made sure to present my project in military terms: a scouting mission to reconnoiter enemy positions. Remarkably, he put up hardly any resistance.

I knew the back way to Karzin now, and again I got there without incident. When I laid out my plan, Hannah Brandt said impulsively, "Libussa, I'm coming with you! You know, they've given us a Polish mayor too, and not even Frau Liebe can get along with him. He showed up here one day, blustered around, and said we didn't belong here anymore and should clear out. Luckily the commandant came along and sent the fellow packing. But now we have an enemy; maybe we'll all have to leave soon. God knows how much longer our good Russians will be here to protect us."

"Our good Russians": what a crazy irony! They had committed murder and arson, and they were responsible for the vast majority of the rapes and lootings. Yet their violence was somehow comprehensible to us, whether we explained it as the principle of an eye for an eye, sheer exuberance, or conquerors' rights. The Poles, on the other hand, were merely camp followers. Their seizure of power had a different character. There was something cold and furtive about it, almost sneaky, which made it seem far more sinister than naked force.

Ten kilometers from Karzin to Stolp; we covered the stretch well before midday. The sign announcing the town's name had been painted over: "Słupsk" it said now, with that little line through the *l*. Our Stolp, our "little Paris," as we had called it fondly, the provincial capital of East Pomerania. Apart from the signs, at first glance not much seemed changed. Bismarckplatz: over there was where Grandmother had lived—my other one, the formidable "Iron Countess." The Iron Chancellor himself was still there, though knocked off his pedestal and beheaded. From fame to scrap metal—*Sic transit gloria mundi.*

The shock came a little later, inside the old city gate: rubble as far as the eye could see, the whole center of the city devastated. Also in ruins, but with its walls still standing, was the mighty brick cathedral, the Marienkirche. The marketplace with its handsome merchants' houses and Mund's Hotel, all gone, gone. Why this devastation? No one had tried to defend the town, so there had been no fighting, just the victors on the rampage.

But we had come not to mourn but to scout the situation. We saw earth-brown uniforms everywhere: Russian military personnel and Polish militia. We stuck to the original inhabitants in their tattered civilian clothes. After five fruitless attempts, we succeeded in getting some information: behind the town hall was an improvised office where Germans could be registered. We found it and joined the queue. After a wait of an hour and a half, we reached the door and were let into a small, bare room with a desk, and behind it a haggard, weary-looking man. He hardly saw us, just stared into space or kept his eyes closed.

"What do you want?" At least the tone of officialdom sounded familiar.

"We wanted to ask about the possibility of emigrating."

"You don't know? Where have you been?"

"In the country, Karzin and Rumbske. No one there has any information. That's why we've come here."

"Ah, the country. So you want to go to Germany, to the Reich?" There it was again, that curious turn of phrase. "You will need authorization from your mayor. He has to attest that there are no charges pending against you."

"But then it will be possible, and the trains are running?"

"That's what I said. Hand luggage only, and provisions for three days."

More we could not get out of him. When we asked for details on the travel conditions, he merely shrugged, drummed his fingers impatiently, and stared straight through us.

Still, we had learned more than we had dared to hope. We boldly decided to ask at the railroad station when trains were departing for the "Reich" and what they were like. But Polish guards turned us away: no admission without papers. We did hear familiar sounds: train bumpers thudding against each other, a locomotive letting off steam.

Hiking back from Stolp took almost twice as long as getting there, not because anyone delayed us but because we kept stopping to discuss what we should do. How difficult it would be to reach a decision! We did not know what the future held if we stayed. And we knew nothing at all about the conditions of emigrating, or what we might find in the "Reich." Any course of action might prove wrong, but there was no way to tell beforehand. Finally, back in Karzin, we developed a plan that could be implemented in stages. First we would go to our respective mayors and procure the necessary papers. Armed with these papers, Hannah Brandt and I would be able to get into the station. And then . . . well, we hoped we would have a clearer sense of the next steps.

SUMMER IN THE GARDENER'S COTTAGE

On the third day, just as promised, I reported back to the gardener's cottage. Strangely, though, my news and plans seemed to arouse little interest. Father Jesko was sitting staring glumly out the window. Mother had a strained air and showed no emotion in her face. What had happened? Had there been a raid or some other disaster? No, nothing of the sort.

I finally took Marie aside and found out that the spinach was to blame. "We had none left, and the baroness—I mean Mother—said, 'We'll have to go and snitch some more from the garden tonight. The baby needs her spinach; she's used to it. We can't wait for Libussa to get back, and besides, it's not fair that we always expect her to do everything.' Then the baron got all upset and said he wasn't going to go creeping around and stealing, and he certainly wouldn't let Mother, either. She didn't say anything, but at night, when he was sleeping, she climbed out the window, and in the morning there was the spinach. He saw it and started yelling at her—all about honor and disgrace, and those sorts of awful things. But this time Mother didn't keep her mouth shut. She said, 'It's not a question of honor, it's a question of the child.' And if need be, she'd do it again. Yes, Libussa, and since then they haven't been speaking to each other."

These Prussians, these German men! So marvelously competent—you could conquer half the globe with them. Pride of office . . . mission . . . duty . . . honor . . . victory! And then in defeat they were suddenly no good for anything, not even stealing spinach, and it was up to us women to make sure the children got fed.

If Father's uniform had been rescued from the Zackenzin pond, if it had been cleaned and put on him, with his medals and ribbons, and if he had been handed a saber and told, "There's the enemy—advance and attack!" that would have presented no problem for him.

I even understood these men. They had been brought up this way, generation after generation. But when it came to ducking your head and crawling on all fours to pick the spinach you needed so as not to starve—with no room for honor and duty—that was where they failed. Such tasks they left to us.

The Gates of Hell, Brandy, and Bread

I was invited to a reception in Hamburg: high society. The guests had heard that I had been in Auschwitz, and a lady asked me, "I suppose you are Jewish?" "No, madam," I replied, "I'm a Polish Catholic." And I realized that even now, twenty years after the war, the Germans had still not understood that the original purpose of Auschwitz was to liquidate the Polish upper class. The idea of gassing the Jews was not implemented until a year and a half later. In Poland, every child knows that. I was shaken to discover that this was news in Hamburg.[12]

A lovelier Sunday morning one could not have wished for. We had had a quiet night, and now I was walking back from the distillery with my well-fed baby. The breeze was warm, not yet hot. Swallows were swooping across the summer sky. Our neighbor's visitor was just untying his horse from the bench. Claudia smiled at him; he laughed, swung himself into the saddle, saluted us, and rode off. The aroma of Marie's carefully husbanded coffee wafted through the window.

But just as we were sitting down to breakfast, a car rolled up to the house. Doors slammed, and three uniformed militiamen came in. Their leader merely said, "Puttkamer?"

Father Jesko slowly got to his feet. "Yes. Baron Puttkamer."

"Under arrest! Come along, this minute!"

He had no time to pack toilet articles or clothes, not even to give us a farewell hug. Tall, slim, and upright, Father Jesko stepped outside, his guards behind him. No wave, hardly a glance back. The doors slammed, the engine started up, and they moved off. A small cloud of dust hovered for a while over the dry road.

Mother sat motionless at the table, as though stunned. She

kept a firm grip on herself—no tears, no lamentations. But I could guess—no, I knew—what was tormenting her. It was not only the pain of separation, concern for her husband's safety, uncertainty as to where fate might take him. It was also violent self-reproach: Might this be the work of the Polish mayor? Should we have stayed in Rowen after all? Would we have avoided this?

We were not left in uncertainty for long. That same day, word came from Glowitz of similar arrests. Then reports arrived from Zemmin, Gutzmerow, and the other villages all around, and within a week it became clear that this was a large-scale operation. Anyone who had held office as a mayor or local farmers' leader, or had enjoyed respect as a master craftsman, innkeeper, or businessman, had been picked up. Father Jesko could not possibly have been spared—whether in Rowen, Rumbske, or anywhere else. Apparently the Poles were systematically eliminating, or at least removing, any men with an ability for leadership who had survived the waves of murders and suicides at the time of the Russian invasion.

The Führer remarked to me: The question of implementing and safeguarding German policy in the Government General is entirely up to the men responsible within the Government General. He expressed himself as follows: What we have identified as the ruling class in Poland is to be liquidated, and any successors that may spring up are to be placed in safekeeping by us and eliminated at the appropriate time. . . . We should not move these elements to concentration camps in the Reich, because that would only create annoyances and unnecessary correspondence with their families; we can liquidate these matters in the country itself. We shall do it in the form that is simplest. Gentlemen, we are no murderers. For the individual policeman, SS man, who must obey his orders to carry out these executions, it is a terrible task. We can easily sign hundreds of death warrants here; but to assign their execution to German men, to decent German soldiers and comrades, is to put a terrible burden on them.[13]

HOUR OF THE WOMEN

Where had they taken Father Jesko, and what had become of him? This uncertainty now hung over everything we did. The only sure thing was that we had to postpone our emigration plans indefinitely. Perhaps Father would be released—tomorrow, the day after, in two weeks or two months. If so, he would need us to be there. If we abandoned him, we would never be able to forgive ourselves. I undertook my third hike to Karzin, so as not to leave Frau Liebe and Hannah Brandt with false hopes.

Rumors flourished, as they always do when reliable information is lacking. First we heard that the arrested men had been taken to Danzig or to Warsaw. Another version had it that the Poles had merely acted on the Russians' behalf, with the prisoners' final destination Siberia. Still other versions, however, mentioned Stolp. Finally, after nearly three weeks, someone told me about a master craftsman in Glowitz who had been picked up at the same time as Father and had since been released. I went to call on him at once. Where had he been held? I asked; had he seen Father?

"You mean our major?"

"Of course."

"Well, they put me in prison in Stolp. It was completely packed, they'd arrested so many people. Ten or twenty of us to a cell, with just two beds—you hardly got to lie down. Practically nothing to eat. And the stench—"

"Yes, but what about the major?"

"I'm getting to that, miss. Well, I didn't actually see him. Not with my own eyes, because they didn't let me out of the cell. But quite a few times I heard people saying, 'Our major's here too, you know.' They all knew him since the march with the Volkssturm."

The first real news, then, and fairly good news, at that. Stolp rather than Danzig, Warsaw, or Siberia. True, you had to check up on a secondhand report like that, lest it, too, become murky and uncertain. One of the man's remarks filled me with consternation: "Practically nothing to eat." I puzzled and puzzled over what to do. I consulted with Mother, and finally I decided to go to Stolp, to the prison. My chances of actually getting to see Father might be slight, but I had to try.

First I went to see Walter Vietzke. He slipped me two small bottles of high-proof liquor. Then Marie got busy baking. With bread and spirits in my rucksack, I set off on my fourth hike to Stolp.

Once more Hannah Brandt showed her courage. "Libussa, I can't let you go by yourself," she said promptly. "I'm coming along." Another night on the now-familiar "Russian cot," and then we set out for the prison.

The large structure behind walls and barbed wire looked as menacing as in earlier times. In the Nazi years it had been the subject of grim rumors; the Gestapo ran it then, torturing "enemies of the Reich," and in principle that could be anyone who did not believe in the Führer and the final victory. The inmates might be different now, but the torture continued.

Outside the gate, women were standing or squatting, hoping for news of husbands, sons, and fathers. They might have a long wait. They simply hung around there passively, making no attempt to get in. After a brief discussion, Hannah and I went up and knocked on the narrow door in the mighty steel gate. A little window slid open, a guard looked out, and we quickly said our piece: "Major Puttkamer—commandant, please." We repeated this several times.

The window shut. Five, ten, maybe twelve minutes elapsed. Then the narrow door opened, and the guard beckoned us through. Involuntarily I took Hannah's hand as the door closed behind us. I thought of Dante at the gates of hell: "Abandon all hope, ye who enter here." A second guard led us across the yard, through passages, and up staircases to the commandant. He leapt up, as though taken by surprise. A red-faced hulk of a man. Standing, he braced his hands on his desk, leaned forward, and bellowed—in Polish, of which we understood not a word. Presumably he meant to intimidate us. Then, quietly and slyly, the question unexpectedly came in German: "General von Puttkamer?"

"No, no, not general, just major."

"Major—with five thousand men?"

"That wasn't with the Wehrmacht, that was the Volkssturm. And he just sent them home again, without combat. And without permission from the Party."

The man made a dismissive gesture, as if to say, "I already know that," or possibly, "That doesn't interest me." I frantically tried to gauge whether this was a good moment to play my trump, the bribe. Well, now or never. As I voiced my request to see Major Puttkamer and bring him some bread, I took out one of the bottles of brandy and placed it on his desk. A short silence, then a glimmer of a smile; the bottle disappeared into a desk drawer. A moment later, the guard was leading us down stairs and through corridors to the cellar. We were taken to a grating, behind which we could more sense than see a long, dark corridor. The only light came from a high cellar window.

"Here wait!" A warden, who was dozing in his chair, lit a barn lantern, unlocked a gate, and locked it again behind him. He clumped off down the corridor. We heard a key rattle, a door crash. We waited.

A man appeared in the gloom, a very old man. Stooped, with bowed head, he shuffled toward us. His hands were clutching a tattered blanket wrapped around his shoulders. Some mistake, surely: this was not Father Jesko.

He came nearer, right up to the grating. Without looking up, he asked in a weary, polite voice, "Yes, what can I do for you?"

No, it was no mistake; I knew this voice. "Father, it's me, Libussa," I managed to say. "I've brought you some bread. Here . . ." I passed it through the bars to him. He took it and immediately bit off a piece.

That was the entire exchange. While the old man chewed and swallowed his bread, I had a lump in my throat. The warden beckoned; he took the prisoner by the arm and led him away. "Father, I'll be back," I managed to call after him. Then we, too, were led away, up stairs, along corridors, and across the yard to the gate. "I'll be back," I said. The guard grinned and slipped my second brandy bottle into his pocket.

I had been prepared for anything, but not for a sight like that. How lucky that Hannah was with me; she dragged me along, through the crowd of waiting women, who rushed up to us excitedly, then fell back again when we did not respond to their questions. Not until we had left Stolp behind did I begin to shake off the numbness, and the next day I actually managed to tell Mother the story in such a way that she felt relieved rather than depressed.

I had my mind made up that I would walk to Stolp every week, to bring Father Jesko his bread; his survival might depend on it. And certainly it was important for me to build up his will to endure. In the long run, though, the stopovers at Karzin would use up much too much time. Going straight to Stolp and spending the night there would save me an entire day. Hannah Brandt came up with a solution: Frau Liebe's ancient cousin, Aunt Melanie, lived on Bahnhofstrasse with her equally ancient housekeeper. Aunt Melanie was hardly of this world anymore; her conversation invariably veered off to life at the court of His Majesty the King of Prussia, Emperor of Germany, as though that were the present. The women now occupied only the front room of the original apartment, and it was crammed with furniture. But summer was here, with balmy nights. They found me a blanket and a pillow, and I spent one night a week curled up on Aunt Melanie's balcony.

Soon my weekly walks to Stolp had become routine. The thirty-odd kilometers in either direction, by way of footpaths that skirted the main road, seemed like nothing at all. The guard at the gate and the commandant received their brandy, and Father got his bread. After a while we even managed to exchange a few more or less natural words. I learned, too, that I had to avoid the heat of day at all costs; one sultry day the loaf was moldy by the time I reached the prison. It stabbed me to the heart to see how greedily Father Jesko took it and bit into it.

Routine always carries a certain risk. When one becomes used to things going smoothly, one tends to let down one's guard. One day I ran straight into three Russians who were lying in a clearing, passing a bottle around.

We stared at one another. One of them slowly got to his feet and swayed toward me, bottle in hand. He held his arms out and said, "Woman, come! Drink! Is good!"

I rammed my knee into his groin as hard as I could. The man bellowed and tumbled to the ground. I took to my heels. No one shot at me, and all that followed me was the braying laughter of his companions.

Ham and Veronal

Things looked very bad in spring,
The fields were bare of everything.
Whatever will the harvest bring?

Those were the first lines of a poem that a girl in a white dress would recite every year at the harvest festival in peacetime. The anxious question was followed by the happy assurance:

Then God sent down his sun and rain,
The fields turned green in warmth of May,
The stalks grew big with ears of grain
That ripened more with each new day.

This year, however, the fields looked even worse in the fullness of summer and the harvest time than in the spring. Human beings in their stupidity had wrecked God's handiwork. Apart from the winter rye and barley, both planted in the autumn, and perhaps a few fields now under Polish control, the only things turning green in the fields were weeds. What little mowing there was had to be done the old way, with a scythe, since the machinery was gone. The situation looked even more grim for Pomerania's principal product, potatoes. The large supplies people had had in root cellars were by now almost exhausted, not least by the demands of the distillery, which the Russians, unlike the Germans, kept going during the summer.

We women in the gardener's cottage at least managed to harvest crops in our own way. You might also say we stole like magpies. As nettles, dandelions, and sorrel became too tough to be suitable for salads and soups, we turned eagerly to the manor garden, drawn there irresistibly by peas and carrots, apples and apricots. Besides, we no longer had anyone to lecture us about "honor" and "disgrace."

Those forays did not always turn out well. One night I slipped through the hole in the wall without having Mother stand guard. I meant to be there for only a few minutes; we had had a storm that afternoon, with powerful wind gusts, and I wanted to fill my basket with fallen fruit.

I had almost finished, when suddenly I heard the shout *"Stoi!"* Straight ahead of me, the Russian sentry stood silhouetted against the evening sky. No time to think; I hurled my basket and its contents in his face as hard as I could. Then I ran off, stooping and weaving. It was an obstacle course through boughs and branches, but their tangled shadows provided cover.

"That's what you get for not being careful," was all Mother said when I returned, out of breath. "And what will we do without our wonderful basket?"

I could not have that on my conscience. Silently, so as not to wake Mother, I slipped out again an hour later; surely the sentry would not be rooted to the spot, and he would probably assume that the thieves had been routed for the night. So now, caution personified, with numerous pauses for looking and listening, I returned to the scene of the crime. The basket was still there: I found it after a short search and did not neglect to fill it again. At home, I left it out on the table, instead of hiding it, as we usually did; and I went to sleep in pleasant anticipation of how my stern baroness would look and what she would say when she saw the basket. But the next morning Mother did not bat an eyelid, only nodded curtly at the basket, as if to say, "That's no more than I would have expected."

As for meat, fat, and eggs, we were really badly off. Rations of the sort we had received during the war no longer existed; we had been put on a crash vegetarian diet. Sometimes I wondered whether I should take up poaching, laying traps deep in the forest, where some deer could still be found. But I could not find any suitable wire, and besides, I had no experience with that kind of thing. All I could recall was the rabbit trap my little brother had designed and built when he was very small. It was a little twig hut with a noose laid out inside, and under it a piece of cardboard with a tack stuck up through it to spike the curious rabbit's nose. My brother was convinced the double device would work better. Actually all the rabbits that got caught in the trap were of the chocolate variety.

Behind August Kuschel's farm, now the residence of the Polish mayor, I discovered a sizable though well-fenced-in flock of chickens. Hiding in the underbrush, I watched how they were locked up for the night in a chicken coop that could hardly be seen from the house because a toolshed stood in the way. What a temptation! I had the necessary equipment for breaking in—a pry bar and a sack—some of the odds and ends I picked up on my foraging expeditions and lugged home, on the principle that you never knew when they might come in handy. And behind our gardener's cottage was a little shed that had long stood empty, just waiting to be used.

I had to wait for a half-moon, which would give me exactly the right amount of light. Twice I was just about to sally forth, when clouds passed over the moon and I could not see. The third time it worked. I was over the fence in a flash, and with no difficulty pried open the rotting door with my bar. The chickens were drowsing and kept still. I quickly stuffed three fine-looking birds into my sack, then took to my heels. Carrying them proved to be not so easy, as they flapped about, but at least they stayed quiet in the sack.

I had chosen well; each of the hens duly laid an egg a day.

Nothing went to waste: I ground up the shells with a stone and put them in Claudia's gruel. We hoped they would give the baby the calcium she needed for her bones and teeth.

The mayor made no secret of his rage, and the whole village was abuzz and quietly chuckling about the bold theft. After three days came an announcement that the militia would conduct a house-to-house search. Great agitation ensued; everyone fortunate enough to have any poultry feared that his own legitimate hens would be confiscated. With great regret, we prematurely put an end to the egg production and performed an emergency slaughter. All traces were carefully removed, the feathers buried in the park. For a week we lived on chicken and delicious broth. It turned out that the threatened search never took place—but how could we have guessed?

No sooner had the excitement and indignation begun to die down than a Russian turned up at our house with a sack over his shoulder. He glanced nervously about and, with unusual politeness, knocked before stepping inside. Using gestures and a few scraps of German, he asked us to look after the sack for him until nightfall. Evidently the man had something on his conscience: "One of those no-good thieves," Marie remarked indignantly, as she popped the last of the chicken bones into the stockpot.

Mother and I merely exchanged glances, then opened the sack, which contained a splendid ham. Without a word, Mother got out the kitchen knife and carved off our share. The ham looked so delicious that our share kept getting larger, in spite of Marie's anxious cry, "Good Lord, Libussa, how are we going to get away with this?" But what thief is in a position to demand restitution if he gets robbed? To make up for the loss in weight, we put a lump of clay in the sack. Even so, our hearts were pounding as night approached. But the darkness did not permit a detailed inspection, and the Russian hastily grabbed his sack, which we had looked after as conscientiously as most receivers of stolen goods. He hurried off, and that was the last we saw of him.

It was a topsy-turvy world: crime worked like magic, while

honest undertakings often failed. We sewed oilcloth pockets into the track suit I wore all the time, so that I could filch things in the shop in Glowitz: a handful of lard, say. Sooner or later, though, I was bound to be noticed, unless I occasionally purchased some item, however small. Certain important things we needed were kept behind the counter—candles, for instance. The days were getting shorter now. But where could I get the zlotys?

I heard that the wife of the mayor of Glowitz was buying valuables. I sought her out, and we began our dealings with a couple of fur items—a muff and a foot warmer—for which I received a pittance. We had a narrow carpet, more a runner actually. I inquired whether the mayor's wife would be interested.

"Of course, of course." In her mind she was already rubbing her hands in anticipation of another bargain.

With the goods rolled up under my arm, I set out. No sooner had I reached Glowitz than I walked straight into the arms of the militia. They arrested me and took me to headquarters. A hearing began, punctuated by threats, shouting, and abuse:

"What's that you've got there?"

"A rug."

"Whose is it?"

"Mine."

"What were you doing with it?"

"Trying to sell it."

"To who?"

"I don't know. I just wanted to ask around and see if anyone was interested." I took pains not to mention the mayor's wife, my only connection.

"Did you know that Germans aren't allowed to sell things?"

"No."

And so on, over and over again. We were getting nowhere. Finally they imposed a double punishment: I had to surrender the carpet without payment or receipt, and I had to stand in the stocks, outside the militia headquarters, on the main street of Glowitz, just a short distance from the church. The day happened to be as hot as in high summer, with the sun baking the wall in front of which I was put on display. Every passerby was entitled to spit at me. But the Poles generally just cleared their throats or spat on the ground, while the Germans crossed to the other side of the street. After about three hours they let me go.

Two days later, I was back in Glowitz. All adults under sixty had been ordered to have a typhoid vaccination. In Mother's case, we simply declared that she was over the age limit, and Marie announced that she was not "feeling well" and had already been exposed to the disease. I was the only one who could not escape.

The program seemed like a good idea. The disease had been raging since spring and reached its climax in the midsummer heat. Hundreds of people had died of typhoid fever, and many doors had a warning sign: "Typhoid." (True, some people used the warning to keep out Russian marauders.) But the epidemic had passed its peak now, and the manner in which the vaccination was carried out made it do more harm than good.

The vaccination station was set up on the street. People waited in long lines while passing trucks raised clouds of dust. Eventually everyone received a stamped certificate–and an injection in the sternum. One needle was used repeatedly; they had no spares, and I saw no evidence that the needle was boiled or disinfected or even wiped off between shots.

Immediately after the injection, a fierce pain shot from my chest to my left arm. I felt dizzy. I could barely drag myself home before I collapsed. Mother had to help me to bed. The pain got worse and worse. I developed a raging fever, accompanied by chills, and my left side became paralyzed; I could not move my arm. At night the pain was almost unbearable, and I asked Mother whether she had anything to help me. After a brief hesitation, she gave me two tablets. They worked, and I finally fell asleep. I slept the rest of the night and the following day and night as well. When I woke up, the pain and paralysis were almost gone, and in the course of the next few days they disappeared altogether.

With my spirits, my curiosity returned. "Mother, what was that you gave me?"

"Veronal."

"Where did you ever get Veronal?"

"That's what they gave Otto-Christoph in his last weeks." That was my real father. He died in 1928 of stomach cancer. Morphine and Veronal gave him a little relief from the excruciating pain at the end.

"Good God, Mother, that was seventeen years ago! And you kept it all this time?"

"Yes. You never know."

True enough: you never know what will happen. One fine day in late summer, the baby was lying in her basket outside the cottage. A Russian came riding up—not Grete's regular visitor. He dismounted, looked at the baby, and picked her up. "Pretty baby," he said. "My Matka, no baby. Matka always sad." He climbed back into the saddle with the baby in his arms and galloped off in the direction of the village.

I dashed out of the house and gave chase just as I was, half dressed and barefoot. The rider was already out of sight, but people in the village pointed the way he had gone. I ran through the village to where the fields began again. And there I saw the man, sitting beside his quietly grazing horse, staring in dismay at the baby, who was yelling her head off. As soon as I got my breath back, I explained that the baby was hungry and absolutely had to be fed. He should come back in the evening for her. He nodded, completely nonplussed.

I hurried home as fast as I could. Altogether, the entire incident had lasted only fifteen minutes or so. And not until it was over and had turned out all right did shock set in; I went limp and began to cry hysterically.

That night, and for several nights and days afterward, we kept the door locked, contrary to our usual practice. I went to bed with my clothes on, ready to jump up at a moment's notice. We hoped to gain time by having Mother fumble with the bolt, while I slid out a back window with the baby and hid in the park. I was convinced, however, that none of this would be necessary; obviously the man had acted on a whim, without thinking of the consequences. He was already a little chastened by the time I caught up with him outside the village. How would he ever take care of a baby until he could go home to Matka? What would his superiors say? By now, we thought, he was probably very embarrassed by what he had done.

But you never know.

Almost a Proper Celebration

"Listen, Libussa," Mother said, "it's time the baby was christened. It's September, and the weather's still fine. Later on in the year, everything will be much more difficult."

She was right, and, as usual these days, her will was our command. The following two weeks were frantically busy—full of problems like great boulders that had to be cleared from our path, one at a time. I still insisted that if we were going to christen Claudia it should be done right, with almost a proper celebration.

First I went to see the pastor in Glowitz: would he do the christening? Of course, but he was afraid to walk the four or five kilometers to Rumbske, so we would have to come to him. All right; after all, we were only women and accustomed to walking. As an unexpected consequence of the kidnaping—which had become the talk of the village—one of the refugee women still living there came to me and tearfully gave me her baby carriage. The baby it had been intended for had died.

Then we brooded over the guest list, which quickly added up to a dozen people. Besides Mother, Marie, and me, the Biedermanns really belonged to the family. Fräulein Rahn had to be there, and Grandma Kreft, her kind landlady. And then Frau Vietzke: her well was running dry now, but without her nursing we would have had no child to christen. Then Frau von Hanstein and her sister from Gutzmerow, and last but not least, Frau Liebe, who had not yet laid eyes on her great-granddaughter, and Hannah Brandt.

Did we really want to be all women, except Uncle Biedermann? Great-Uncle Gerhard, the old Glowitzer, came to mind. A witness at my wedding, he could now stand in for my brother as Claudia's godfather. But Marie protested, almost in a frenzy: "No, Libussa, you can't invite him! Absolutely not!"

"Good Lord, why not?"

"Because that would make thirteen at table. That's unlucky. You can't do that to our poor innocent child."

Nothing would change her mind, so she had her way. I had to content myself with inviting Great-Uncle Gerhard to the ceremony in Glowitz.

Next came the problem with Karzin. Inviting my grandmother and Hannah simply involved a detour the next time I went to Stolp. But how would my eighty-two-year-old grandmother ever get to Rumbske? She was more than willing to attempt the long walk, but Hannah Brandt put her foot down. A few hours later, when I stopped by on my way back from Stolp, the problem was solved: Frau Liebe had had a word with "her" commandant, and he had promised her a horse and cart, with a soldier to act as escort and driver.

When Marie heard that, she could hardly believe it: thirteen people again, and the thirteenth a Russian! Using contradictory arguments—that on the one hand the coachman did not really count as a guest, and on the other hand the baby Claudia herself was the fourteenth person—I managed to placate her somewhat. What finally brought her around, though, was the prospect of riding to church in the cart, rather than pushing the baby carriage all the way.

It turned out to be relatively easy to round up chairs, plates, cups, knives, and forks. Whatever we lacked, we could borrow from Grete Krupps and Frau Vietzke. And we still had a damask tablecloth for Marie's heirloom.

Silver would of course look better on the damask than our

everyday flatware. We wondered what had become of our buried treasure. It had completely slipped my mind, but the occasion jogged my memory. The underground passage to the Octagon and the slaughter room should still be intact; it led away from the house and therefore would not have been buried under collapsing walls. The assumption proved correct; without difficulty I got into the abandoned tunnel, followed it to the slaughter room, and found—a gaping hole. Others had dug here long since; too many people must have known or guessed where to look. I felt disappointed and ashamed: the Klenzin secret from the Thirty Years' War had endured for three centuries, ours probably no more than three weeks. All I found were two teaspoons, dropped in the sand, and the pickax left behind by the treasure hunters.

The problem of what to eat seemed almost insoluble. Yet according to Pomeranian tradition, the food was supposed to be the centerpiece and climax of the celebration. Without a festive meal, a celebration did not deserve the name; it was doomed to fail. An empty stomach weighs on the heart and the spirits. No one knew that better than Marie, who wailed and moaned. She was quite prepared to empty out her barrel of salted meat, but by now it contained only scraps. And how much flavor could they have, even after thorough soaking?

In the end, this problem, too, found an unexpected solution. For some time now, a group of German POWs had been housed in the loft of the distillery. They had been put to work chopping down trees in the park; the beech and oak logs would keep the distillery fires burning. Every morning on their way to work they marched past our cottage. They were not very closely guarded, and we managed to slip the men fresh fruit, of which we had a plentiful supply at the moment. Of course, word got around of our project, and of the attendant difficulties. Just four days before the day, on their way back from work, the prisoners waved to me, and one of them pulled something from under his jacket and flung it into the bushes. No sooner had the men and their guard passed than I went to the spot and found a fully grown, autumnally plump hare!

Had they trapped it or ambushed it coming out of its hole? Whatever the case, Marie positively beamed when I brought it to her. She pooh-poohed my concern as to whether thirteen people—or rather, twelve guests plus a coachman—could be fed with one rabbit: "Just leave it to me." Soon an enormous cauldron turned up, borrowed from somewhere, and Mother and I were banished from the kitchen. Marie wanted to surprise us.

The great day arrived. We moved Marie's bed out of the sitting room into the back room, the chairs arrived, a few at a time, and we decorated the room with the roses that still bloomed bravely in the beds along the drive to our former manor. Then came the clip-clop of horses' hooves—the cart from Karzin. But no, by God, no cart but a real carriage, drawn by two horses, with a young soldier sitting on the box, announcing his arrival with exuberant cracks of the whip.

After a quick breakfast, we rode off to Glowitz, where another surprise awaited us: the church was full of people, almost like my wedding. They had streamed in from Rumbske and Rowen and God knows where, to watch, to join us in celebration, to comfort each other. The church still provided a refuge, as it always had.

The old Glowitzer had aged; he was rather shaky now but calmer and gentler, not to say more tender; he solemnly embraced me in front of the whole congregation. He still had his ancient hat and stick, and when the time came, he held the baby firmly. Frau Liebe, as the godmother, stood beside him.

The old custom of walking around the altar with the baby, then the benediction, the singing, and finally a prayer . . . By the end, hardly an eye was dry.

> Almighty and everlasting God, our loving Heavenly Father, we thank Thee for giving us this child Claudia, for keeping her safe from harm and allowing her to go forth from Holy Baptism to be reborn into eternal life and

> union with Thy Son, our Lord Jesus Christ. We humbly beseech Thee to accept this child as Thine heir, that she may be brought up in the light of Thy grace and remain in the one true Faith all her life, then to receive her promised inheritance with all Thy Saints in Heaven, through Jesus Christ our Lord. Amen!

As we left the church, a murmur ran through the congregation: "Look at that carriage, with the Ivan on the box!" Yes, it certainly was odd. On the way back to Rumbske, my thoughts involuntarily returned to that summer day barely fifteen months earlier, with the man at my side in his steel helmet and field-gray uniform. What had become of him? And now, after the collapse of that world, this other, autumnal drive, with that other, earth-brown uniform before me.

A babble of voices and laughter: eleven German women, old Uncle Biedermann, and a young Russian.

After looking back and forth between the newly christened babe and her great-grandmother, Grandma Kreft shook her head and characteristically spoke her mind: "No, ma'am, it's not you she takes after. But she's the spittin' image of old Elisabeth!" By which she meant the other grandmother, the "Iron Countess" Krockow. Frau Liebe accepted it with composure.

And now Marie's hour of glory had arrived. Her "feast" consisted only of a stew. But what a stew! Rabbit stew, flavored with all sorts of herbs. No one could recall having eaten anything so delicious. Of course, there were potatoes to go with it, and carrots, and everything in sufficient quantity, so that the guests could confidently be urged to have seconds. Ivan, as he was actually named, filled his plate six times. For dessert we had stewed apricots, and we finished with freshly roasted coffee; today the cups were replenished without concern for our dwindling supply. And Frau Vietzke provided a dollop of brandy in every cup. Grandma Kreft came up with an apt comment, as always: "Well, that calls for a good belch!"

The company grew animated, with people talking a blue

streak. Frau Vietzke proudly explained to my Karzin grandmother how it came about that her baby and Claudia had survived while the other three babies born in Rumbske that year had all died. Finally we sang—lullabies for the almost forgotten little person we were celebrating, and the "kitchen songs" that Marie adored, so beautiful that they sent shivers down our spines. But Ivan outdid us all. He had thought to bring his balalaika with him, and accompanied his melancholy Slavic songs on it.

Hannah Brandt was the only one who did not quite lose track of time. "My goodness," she exclaimed, "it's already getting dark; we must be on our way!" Silence suddenly settled over the company. Then Frau Liebe stood up and recited the last strophe of Matthias Claudius's beautiful "Evensong":

So lay ye down, my brethren,
In the name of God in heaven,
The evening's breath blows chill.
Oh, spare us, Lord, be keeping
Us all the while we're sleeping,
And our neighbor who is ill.

Lights in the Darkness

Farewell to the Biedermanns

The Biedermanns were making ready to leave. They wanted to, they had to be off. Winter was almost upon us, the days growing shorter and shorter. They had only their summer clothes, by now shabby and threadbare. Uncle Biedermann was still wearing his trademark knickerbockers and white linen jacket. Of a Sunday, he would sometimes add a bow tie, as if to defy circumstances with a touch of elegance. But his shirt collar was pathetically frayed, the jacket, now more gray than white, barely held together with patches, and the bottoms of his knickerbockers flapped around his legs, because the elastic in the bands had given up the ghost.

But the critical factor was that we could no longer feed the Biedermanns. They still turned up for lunch and supper in our cottage, having had for breakfast the bit of bread we had given them the night before, with perhaps a little syrup or whatever their landlady or someone else happened to supply. Aunt Deten would arrive looking reproachful in advance, because she knew there would not be enough for her Albrecht again. But the stocks Marie had taken along on the trek were now all but exhausted. We had no idea how we would get through the winter ourselves. And the Biedermanns' little room, or rather windowless closet, in the village could not be heated; sooner or later they would freeze to death there.

Months before, Hannah Brandt and I had found out that trains were running again between Stolp and Stettin, and that transports departed almost daily for those wanting to go west, to make room for the Poles, who were arriving here in ever-increasing numbers. Fräulein Trautmann was not the only one to have braved the trip home "to the Reich." More and more we heard of people who had left, either going home, like the evacuees from the Ruhr, or leaving home for places new and unfamiliar.

First the Biedermanns had to get a ride to Stolp. But that should be possible, for a lot of traffic was going back and forth these days. As so often, Walter Vietzke provided invaluable assistance: in return for a bottle of almost pure alcohol, diverted from the distillery's output, a Polish driver promptly agreed to add a couple of quiet passengers to his load of squealing pigs.

I had a letter, written earlier but not sent off. Now I added a postscript and asked the Biedermanns to take the packet with them. For writing materials I had had to apply to Emil Priedigkeit, once the proprietor of the general store, now the "exproprietee," as we jokingly called him. Though forced out of his shop into smaller premises, he still had a few precious items on hand, like paper, ink, and pens. To think that we had once taken such things for granted!

This was not my first letter, nor would it be my last. I had tried repeatedly to send word to the west, hoping for a reply. After all, the Polish postal service had been operating for some time now. But apparently none of my letters had reached their destination; at least I had not received any replies. This one proved the exception—hence its survival.

Rumbske, 7 Sept. 1945

Dearest M.,

I have written to you a couple of times already, but I am not sure whether my letters ever reached you. This time our Glowitz pastor is going to try to get to Berlin, and I shall ask him to send this on its way. Supposedly there are fairly safe trains now from Stolp to Berlin, i.e., trains where you are not robbed of everything, down to the shirt on your back (one of the more harmless features of life in our zone). M., if you want to try, write me at this new Polish version of our address: *wies Rumsko, poviat Słupsk, Pomorze.* Słupsk, with that line through the *l,* is supposed to mean Stolp. I have heard that even letters addressed in German arrive, though I have yet to see one. Try it both ways, if you like.

We do not yet know whether we are German or Polish—no news has come from the outside world since the end of March. They say the war is over, but we have had no confirmation. For us, at any rate, it is still in full swing. We have almost exhausted the last of our supplies. We now live on stolen potatoes and anything else we manage to beg or steal. We have come a long way! Meat, sausage, and such can no longer be had—the prize question these days is: how many different ways can you cook potatoes? The little one is so delicate, almost six months old now, but what am I going to give her to eat? The prospect of winter haunts us. . . . Father in prison in Stolp for the last three months.

Beginning of October

The pastor never went, having heard that conditions were worse than ever on the trains. As far as the Oder (the Polish border), it is like traveling in the Middle Ages: you arrive barefoot and stripped to your underwear—if you are lucky. Nevertheless, the Biedermanns, whom we have provided for until now, are setting out for Berlin this week. We can no longer feed them. We are laboriously gathering fuel in the park for winter. We have "organized" an ax and a saw and are cutting down trees—no easy task when there are no men around to help. Still no news, only wild rumors as to our future. Father still in prison in Stolp. I walk there every week to bring him bread—our branch line has been dismantled. For the last fortnight there has been no milk for the baby—until then there was half a liter a day for children, nothing for adults. Now I steal milk too, every morning. It is a dangerous business—you take your life in your hands, but the child is the main thing, and she has to have milk. Children are dying of malnutrition every day. As long as I can find a way, I do not mind what it is. And she is so happy, laughing and making a racket all day. If we did not have her, we might have given up the struggle.

If you had received any of my previous letters, you would more or less know the course our life has taken. I doubt I will ever go through anything as terrible and difficult as long as I live. Our house is no longer standing. Most of the local landowners are dead. We are living in what used to be the gardener's cottage, in two rooms and a kitchen, and it seems palatial to us, compared to other places we have lived in during the last six months. My baby, your goddaughter, by the way, is called Claudia Christina Emmy. She was born on March 23, in an attic. For thirty-seven hours our lives hung in the balance, but we got through that all right, and quite a few other things besides, when we were sure our last moment had struck.

Yes, M., we often speak of you, and of the possibility of taking refuge with you. But first, we do not want to leave without Father, and second, the baby cannot survive a journey under the present conditions, and third, we have had no news of you and yours—how you have fared, if it is more peaceful where you are. If at all possible, please write!

Saying goodbye to the Biedermanns was not easy; tears flowed on both sides. As far back as I could remember, the Biedermanns were associated with summer in Rumbske. Viewed objectively, they actually spent six months of the year sponging off the owners of various Pomeranian estates. He was a landscape and still-life painter of no particular distinction. His wife, impoverished, like so many, by the inflation in the twenties, became a believer in miracles, then in Hitler. They would show up in Rumbske at the beginning of July and stay until September; as evidence of purposeful activity, Uncle Biedermann would set up his easel outdoors, especially in the wake of a downpour, when flocks of clouds would be mirrored in the puddles in a wagon track: "Uncle Biedermann weather," we called this. The pictures gradually filled the whole house.

But what a delight Uncle Biedermann was for us children! We always waited impatiently for him to arrive, because in his hands toys that had broken over the course of the year would miraculously become whole again. "Undel Biedelmann, please fix horsey"—with those words, my brother would expectantly hold out his wooden horse that had lost its head. Uncle Biedermann would carve a new head and glue it on. He constructed entire farmyards, created beautifully painted armor and Red Indian outfits. He would even allow us to tie him to the stake and did not object when we left him there; Aunt Deten had to go out at dusk to find him. She would wander through the park calling "Albrecht! Albrecht!" in her jarring voice. If a rainy afternoon threatened to suffocate us with boredom, Uncle Biedermann would improvise games, or he would fascinate us with his puppet theater—also homemade, of course. The finale was always the "Chinese chorus":

In China it's bad
When one of the Chinese
Who's been stealing like mad,
Has his belly slit open, if you please . . .

We acted this out, leaping in the air and crashing down, with gestures and sounds, making it as drastic and bloody as possible.

When Aunt Deten was in a good mood, she, too, would contribute to the entertainment; she loved to tell East Prussian stories and recite poetry in broad local dialect.

But now it was farewell to the two old people, heading off into the unknown—Uncle Biedermann with a rucksack on his narrow shoulders and a little suitcase held together with a length of string. What would become of them? What we knew of conditions on the trains—or rather, what had percolated through to us as rumor—is documented in my letter. Would they even survive the journey? Or end up in a camp and die a miserable death? And if they actually reached Berlin, would their apartment in Steglitz still be there? And wasn't hunger spreading a pall over the ruins of what had once proudly been called the capital of the Reich? So many questions, and no answers. Two old people, stiff, almost petrified, as the driver cracked his whip. No waving, no shouted farewells. Just the squealing of the pigs, creatures crying in distress—but even that not for long.

Glowing Embers Amid the Coals

How many times had I walked to Stolp to bring Father his bread? I had not kept track, so routine had it become; my walk to the prison simply formed part of my week. That made the shock, when it came, all the worse. After a cagey look around, the guard at the gate pocketed his bottle, but then did not let me in: "Father gone," he said. "Many gone—Gdansk."

"What—to Danzig?"

"Yes, Gdansk."

I managed to get in to speak to the commandant. He confirmed what I had heard at the gate, and seemed friendly enough: "Full investigation there. Don't be sad. Much better there. Heat in winter. Not possible here. Goodbye. *Do widzenia!*"

I was left at a loss. Maybe things really were "better" there, maybe not. What did the commandant know? Had he ever been in Danzig, did he have any firsthand knowledge of conditions? Probably his assurances were platitudes, the kind of thing specialists would say to a gravely ill patient to conceal the seriousness of his condition; perhaps he had read the horror in my eyes.

Two things now seemed certain. First, we could not count on Father Jesko's returning anytime soon. Why else would they have gone to the trouble of transferring him? Terms like "full investigation" and "winter" spoke for themselves. Second, Father was now out of reach. True, ordinary passenger trains did run occasionally, but everyone knew that Germans were strictly prohibited from using them. Besides, I did not have the zlotys for a ticket. And walking to Danzig was out of the question. It was not thirty kilometers but over a hundred, through completely unfamiliar country, where I had no friends or relations, nowhere to spend the night and rest. No, it could not be done. Besides which, my bread, with its tendency to go moldy, set strict limits on the distance I could cover. Now we women had no choice but to prepare to get through the winter on our own, as best we could.

"The prospect of winter haunts us," I had written in my letter, and that was no exaggeration. The months ahead terrified us. We found ourselves facing something that had been well known in the so-called good old days but that pride in our progress toward modern civilization had allowed us to lose sight of. As it said in an old songbook,

As all around the fields lie bare,
And over them the cold fogs fare,
And frost bedecks the mowing:
Thus perish all our worldly joys,
Life's strength and splendor seem but toys,
Death's shadows swiftly growing.

In East Pomerania, before the war, winter was a time of tempting aromas: apples baking in the oven, sausages, hams, and goose breast curing in the smokehouse, freshly roasted coffee, and gingerbread. Winter was the season of the great hunts, with ensuing festive *dîners,* or, as we jokingly called them, "platter hunts." Ice skates came into their own on the frozen village pond, toboggans on the slope in the foals' paddock. It was a time for rides in horse-drawn sleighs, with clouds of steam from the horses' nostrils billowing over us, and the bells jingling merrily. Who minded the cold? We bundled up in furs from head to foot. For the peasants, winter meant a respite from the hard work of the rest of the year, from spring plowing to the autumn potato harvest. And winter meant Christmas.

We humans' casual and even affectionate relationship with winter depends on something fundamentally unnatural: the triumph of progress, which skims along on the thin ice of a smoothly functioning order. It presupposes our mastery of nature. Woe unto us when that mastery suddenly collapses and our power turns to powerlessness. Suddenly everything changes, and the cozy season of early lamplight and blazing fires becomes dark, threatening, and elemental.

Human existence must have been like this for hundreds and thousands of years in our part of the world, except that we had forgotten it. At one time winter brought severe limitations. Man and beast alike faced hardship. In agriculture there was the term "tail cattle," for animals too weak to get on their feet after the deprivations of winter. In the spring they had to be dragged out to pasture by their tails. Human beings were threatened by deficiency diseases like scurvy, because they had no fresh fruits or vegetables. Another danger was rickets; among the terrors of my childhood was the spoonful of cod-liver oil administered daily in winter to avert the "English disease." But even that was idyllic compared to the situation we faced in the fall of 1945.

Our first priority had to be to protect ourselves against the cold, against the danger of freezing. We were fortunate to have a good stove. It drew well, and when the doors were kept shut, it held its heat for hours. Unfortunately, it needed to be fed with firewood. Our cottage, located outside the village, backed up on the park, with its dense growth of beeches. Fallen branches and twigs were plentiful; we had only to collect them. But while they were fine for a crackling open fire, they would not keep the stove going for long periods.

Still, during the summer I had made an important acquisition. While out scouring the countryside for usable items, I came upon the main barn at Rowen. It was locked, but under the doors were grooves worn over the years by the harvest wagons. One was deep enough so that I could wiggle my way in. The barn was full of implements: plows and harrows, a roller. There I found things that made my heart leap for joy: an ax and a saw. But if anyone caught me with my booty, I would be in deep trouble. So I crept into a stack of straw in the farthest, darkest corner and waited, half dozing, half listening, until darkness fell and I could return home in triumph.

Handling an ax and a saw to cut down trees and saw them up, carrying or rolling the logs to the back of the house, splitting them, and stacking woodpiles in such a way that the wind could dry the logs but the rain would stay out—all these were difficult and unfamiliar tasks for us. We began in the summer and continued through the autumn and the entire winter.

One time a storm blew over a birch tree on the edge of the village pond, and it fell directly across the path from our house to the distillery. I hurried there with the saw. Although beech generates more warmth, because it is dense, the lighter birch is good for getting a fire going. As I knelt on the ground, sawing away, I suddenly saw a pair of boots standing in front of me. Slowly I looked up—and froze in horror. It was the Russian commandant. Cutting down trees—like almost everything else—was strictly prohibited. Of course, I had not cut the tree down, but it was his word against mine, and how easily he could take away my irreplaceable saw! And wasn't stealing firewood bad enough?

The commandant shook his head with a half-amused, half-reproachful smile. He said, "Now look, that's no way to saw up a log!" Then he showed me the proper way to do it, how to prop the trunk so it would not bind. He helped me until the birch was all sawed up.

The commandant's name was Sasha, or at least that was what he was called. He was a young and cultivated man, a medical student from Moscow, who spoke good German. The next day he paid us a visit. Of course he knew who we were; that was why he wanted to come and talk. We sacrificed almost the last of our coffee, to which our guest added a little vodka; the conversation lasted until far into the evening.

Sasha loved Heine. He longed to see the Rhine, with its vineyards, cliffs, and ruined castles; he recited "The Lorelei," and it sounded all the more expressive in his Russian accent:

I cannot explain the sadness
That's fallen on my breast.
An old, old fable haunts me,
And will not let me rest.[14]

He was dumbfounded when we told him that in the Third Reich, songbooks had listed this poem as "Folk song, author unknown," because Heine was a Jew. We recited a poem called "The Handstand on the Lorelei," written before our present great epoch by Erich Kästner. Based on a true incident, the poem describes a German "hero," who flaunts his courage in the spirit of the nationalistic nineteenth-century German gymnastics enthusiast "Turnvater" Jahn:

He thought of Heine's lovely Lorelei,
And down he plummeted
And broke his neck . . .

"Ah," said Sasha, less triumphant than melancholy, "and there they lie, these heroes, quite broken. . . . And have the survivors learned anything? But my Heine, your unknown poet, he always warned against that nationalistic father of gymnasts and his gymnast sons." A young Russian and two German women reciting poems to each other and discussing the abysses of German culture: that, too, was part of the autumn of 1945.

A little later, we suffered another night break-in. We lost our big footlocker, which we had been using as a wardrobe—one of those enormous, wood-ribbed objects made to last forever, which people used to take on journeys, apparently thinking they had to have half their household with them. Impulsively, I went straight to the commandant and reported the theft. And lo: he tracked down the trunk—though not its contents, which were actually far more important to us—and brought it back to us, beaming.

Alas, Sasha was replaced after a few weeks; he represented the one exception in a long line of commandants. A more typical one received the sobriquet "Dark Night" as a result of his fondness for nocturnal raids.

A second story connected with our firewood gathering reached me more than forty years later, in 1986, from Australia. A former resident of our area wrote:

> My mother, my younger brother, and I went into the forest to gather wood. There we came upon your mother and her maid, kneeling on the ground, sawing. My mother greeted her and said, "Baroness, it distresses me to see you having to work this way." Your mother stood up, straight as a ramrod, and replied, "Frau Bielang, one must face fate with one's head held high." This encounter made such an impression on me—still a child at the time—that it has remained with me ever since. In the dark hours of my life, it has come back to me and raised me up.

That was Mother. In accordance with the ideals instilled by her upbringing, and her personal convictions as well, she always remained in control of herself, determined never to succumb to self-pity and always to keep her feelings to herself. She abhorred emotional people, calling them "bleeding hearts." If one did not know her, one might easily mistake her attitude for coldness, which it most certainly was not. It was dignity—ramrod straight in every sense, in every situation, into ripe old age. "There goes Prussia," I once heard a stranger remark as he watched my mother pass. In all those years, those decades of our living and being together, I saw her break down and cry only twice: the first time was in September 1939, when she received word that her eldest son had died as a young officer outside Warsaw; the second time was when, after that long struggle between life and death in the attic in Rowen, her granddaughter finally gave her first cry.

The daily battle for survival often turned on absurdly trivial things—matches, for instance. Our supply was dwindling, with the prospects for replenishing it slim. So everything depended on our keeping the stove going through the night. Easy enough with coal, not so with wood. Usually we managed by carefully banking the fire with ashes.

But apparently some little kobold made it his business to see that our stove and Grete Krupps's next door always went out at the same time. When that happened, embers had to be transported either from the distillery or from the nearest dwelling, carried at a gallop in an old bucket with a piece of tin on top to guard the embers from drafts.

The things one learns when one has to! The beech ash, for instance, served another purpose: it replaced laundry powder for us. It might not produce a dazzling white wash, but it did get things more or less clean.

Gardens of Eden; or, the Fruits of Self-restraint

Keeping our rooms warm might be hard work, but it was not a serious problem. There was plenty of wood available; it just had to be collected. Food was another matter. We had no rations and no money with which to buy anything, and we could no longer get nettles or sorrel for soup or dandelions for salad. Playing cops-and-robbers in the manorial garden had become pointless. That we survived the winter was a matter of lucky circumstances.

First of all, the distillery proved invaluable. The Russians insisted on keeping it going and saw to it that a steady supply of potatoes was brought in, first from the immediate vicinity and then, when that ran out, from farther away. Because they considered *kultura* important, the Russians wanted the potatoes not only washed but also peeled. So day after day a throng of women gathered around an enormous tub to do this essentially unnecessary work, as if to feed an army. They received no wages. Instead, the women eagerly filled hidden pockets with peelings and a small supply of the precious vegetables, although this was strictly forbidden. For some time now, Marie had been working at the distillery. Thus we procured the staple of the Pomeranian diet, introduced in the days of Frederick the Great.

Our second stroke of good fortune came in the form of Herr and Frau Gleumann, owners of the mill at Klenzin. Perhaps we had done something special for them in earlier times; in any case, the Gleumanns now proved themselves loyal friends. The mill stood at a slight distance from the other houses in the village, on its millstream. It, too, was kept busy, and supplied with grain. The victors needed flour as much as the defeated. About twice a month, Mother or I would sneak off in the dusk, taking a four-kilometer roundabout route that brought us to the Gleumanns' back door under cover of darkness. And we never went away empty-handed. They always filled our little bags with flour and semolina. Nor would Frau Gleumann let us leave without a piece of bread with something on it, "to fortify" us for the walk.

Third, there was the "Garden of Eden." No one knew where the name originated, but it referred to a rather neglected little apple orchard in a remote corner of the park. The twisted old trees had not borne much fruit in recent years, but in this grim autumn they produced plentifully. And there were neither cherubim with bared swords nor Russians with submachine guns to block our entrance to the garden.

So on a succession of moonlit nights, we returned to this Garden of Eden. I clambered up and shook the trees, while Mother and Marie gathered the fruit. But we were not always alone. One time I almost fell to the ground in fright when I saw a dark shape crouched above me in the tree I was climbing. It turned out to be a village boy, as tempted by the apples as we were. Our mutual alarm soon gave way to whispers and suppressed giggles. That night the boy did all the shaking, and we gave him his share.

Fourth, a guardian angel appeared, Herr Totta, the Pole who had taken over Wilhelm Lemke's farm. I do not recall whether he was already living in Rumbske before the Russians came, as a POW or a forced laborer, or only arrived later. In any case, he was here now, and he had a soft spot in his heart for us, especially Claudia. This man with his slight build and his sly smile had either kept or managed to acquire a thing of great value: a cow with an excellent milk supply.

The milk ration for infants was cut off in the autumn. Not only that: because of the overall shortage, it was made a crime to supply any milk to Germans. *"Verboten! Verboten!"* That was the harsh word we constantly encountered in our struggle to survive. But stealing milk—in other words, secretly milking cows at night—had become much more difficult, indeed almost impossible, since with the onset of cold weather the remaining livestock had been moved indoors.

Precisely at this critical juncture Herr Totta offered to help. Of course, I could go only after dark. But that came early enough now, and since the Lemke or Totta farm lay on the edge of the village, I could easily get there without being seen. I still had a few nice shirts of Jobst's, which I took one at a time to Herr Totta. He was happy to accept them, but I am sure he would have given me my milk even if I had had nothing for him.

Last but not least, I must sing the praises of our Marie. Our beloved cook had been accustomed to working with a full larder. During World War I she had come to Rumbske as a fifteen-year-old, shortly after my mother arrived, and she had learned her craft at the manor. No one had ever trained her to make do with nothing. Now she carried it off with flair. How many ways could you prepare potatoes and apples, or apples and potatoes? Marie conjured up everything, from soups to purées to casseroles, so that we often found ourselves eating with pleasure, not just to still our hunger. "Our Marie would make shoe leather taste good!" we exclaimed whenever she concocted something new. A particular highlight were her sweet desserts, which her sack of sugar still made possible occasionally.

But of course we rationed the sugar with Spartan self-restraint. Likewise the few apples that lasted into the new year. Fat we had only when I snitched some from the shop in Glowitz. And meat remained the extraordinary exception. The Gleumanns, whose allotments and output were scrupulously weighed, were taking a great risk in letting us have anything at all. So we still had to use ground birch bark in our dough and bake it with distillery yeast.

Curiously enough, though our stomachs might rumble long and loud that winter, we never suffered from digestive troubles. Moldy bread, frostbitten potatoes, bad-smelling meat that the Russians occasionally gave the women working at the distillery—none of this made us sick. Ironically, we had been put on an involuntary but very successful diet. Mother in particular had always had a delicate stomach, from the time she was a girl. Now her episodes of nausea, diarrhea, constipation, and lack of appetite were gone, never to return.

Not by Bread Alone

"But the children of the kingdom shall be cast out into outer darkness: there shall be weeping and gnashing of teeth," it says in the Gospel According to Saint Matthew. Darkness, truly and literally: Rumbske lay as far north as Königsberg in East Prussia, so in winter it got dark at four o'clock and stayed dark until well into the following morning.

Darkness ruled absolutely. Comforts we had once taken for granted seemed like a remote dream: we had no electric light, no fuel for lamps or lanterns, no wax candles or tallow lights.

The lack of light posed a serious problem: the baby could not go sixteen hours without food. She needed an evening meal, but how could we see to feed her? We recalled that the old Germanic tales mentioned *Kienspäne*. These were wood splinters soaked in pine pitch that served as torches. We decided to make our own. With Father's hunting knife we cut gashes in pine trunks and wedged splinters of wood into them. After a while they were sticky and impregnated with resin.

But the ancient Germans must have known something we did not, for our pine splinters produced only a sputtering glow. They also produced generous amounts of soot, which more often than not fell in flakes into the baby's gruel. But the flickering was enough for our eyes, accustomed now to darkness, and the soot seemed not to harm the baby.

The darkness itself, however, became more and more of a problem for us adults. One cannot spend two thirds of the day and night asleep or hibernating—a human being is not a dormouse. Still less can one sit and stare into space. Darkness darkens the soul; involuntarily our thoughts turn to calamities and dire things: the next raid was imminent and would be especially brutal; perhaps Father had already died of cold or hunger; if the baby got sick, she would die, because we had no doctor and no medicine; soon we would have nothing left to sell; our last provisions were almost used up. And so on and so forth.

So we needed something to occupy our minds, a kind of survival therapy. We had only one possibility: pine splinter in hand, so to speak, we had to descend into the labyrinthine corridors and vaults of memory, and search for treasures that the rust of time had coated but not yet eaten away. Fortunately, we still belonged to those generations for whom learning poetry by heart and reciting it formed an integral part of our schooling and growing up. Looking back on our experiences as treasure hunters, I sometimes wonder what the children of today would do in similar circumstances. Would the passages of their memories turn up anything more than the useless ghosts of Superman or Donald Duck?

In the first vault we came upon classic ballads. Goethe, from "The Erlking" to "The Magician's Apprentice," Schiller, from "The Diver" to "The Pledge," Uhland's "Swabian Tidings" and "The Singer's Curse," Chamisso's "Giants'

Plaything," Bürger's "Leonore"—we knew them all, as well as we knew the multiplication tables. These ballads had one great virtue: they lent themselves wonderfully to dramatic, even spine-chilling recital. Mother excelled at this. In her eagerness to perform at her best, she would involuntarily stand up—in the dark—as though she were still a schoolgirl at the turn of the century, reciting with glowing enthusiasm to her classmates.

Of course we ran into occasional hitches too.

The wind of spring blew from the sea
And blustered wet and grim through France.

That was the beginning of Gottfried August Bürger's "Song of the Good Husband," but how did it go on? As in this ballad about a spring flood destroying a bridge and threatening to drown the customs officer and his wife and child, so we often wandered among ruins in our memory, uncertain as to whether they could still be pieced together. But under all the dust and rubble, far more remained intact than we would have believed; and the harder we looked, the more frequently we succeeded in finding things we would not have expected to recover. Indeed, much of the delight, and the actual purpose of our activity, lay in the search. Once activated, memory continued to work on its own, preventing our thoughts from plunging into fears of approaching disaster. Quite often, an afternoon session would begin right where we had left off the previous night, with the remark, "You won't believe it, but last night I suddenly remembered . . ." Soon we ceased to marvel, and accepted these feats of memory as perfectly natural.

Gradually we managed to put together quite a repertory. Inevitably, some mistakes crept into our versions, particularly once we left the ballad for territory where there was no dramatic story line to carry us along:

Head bending over a sermon book, beside him the cozy fire,
Sat the virtuous Tamm . . .

That was the beginning of a long poem in classical meter by Johann Heinrich Voss, called "The Seventieth Birthday." But try as we would, we could not get beyond those first lines. The same held true for Seume's poem on the noble savage. Only the phrase "Old Europe's veneer of politeness" was still there, and of course the marvelous ending:

Calmly smiling spoke the Huron then:
"See, you clever, pale-faced foreigners,
Though savages, we are the better people!"
This said, he slipped into the bushes.

We failed with Schiller's "The Bell" for quite another reason. The poem gave us no trouble until we reached the line "indoors the housewife with industry labors." Mother suddenly stopped me and declared peremptorily, "No, that's simply too silly for words." With that, this particular bell was summarily melted down.

Some memory vaults we never set foot in, however much seemed to be stored in them. With a few exceptions, we bypassed lyric poetry, perhaps because it might bring us perilously close to the vortex of strong feeling. But most particularly we shunned the heroic patriotic poetry that had played such a prominent role in our school days; in Mother's youth, the anniversary of the Battle of Sedan formed the high point in the national calendar. What good to us now were poems like "The Ems Dispatch," "The Trumpeter of Gravelotte," or "God Who Made the Iron Grow"? What was the point of a "call echoing like thunder," and where had that "Germania" led her children in the end? No, no, without even discussing it, we refused to touch that bombastic patriotic stuff. For it had not survived, and it could offer us no help with survival.

But humor, and intentional and unintentional comedy, played a large, sometimes dominant role. "After a lost war, comedies should be performed," the Austrian poet Hofmannsthal once wrote. How true! One can respond to a catastrophe by laughing as well as by crying. The poems of

Christian Morgenstern, Wilhelm Busch, and Friederike Klempner provided an almost inexhaustible stock of laughter.

To be sure, Marie did not really understand our sense of humor. Sometimes she was outraged by something that made us laugh, and then we would have to placate her. But she made her own contribution with her wonderfully sentimental "kitchen songs," like "Mariechen sat weeping in the garden" or "Why dost thou weep, O gardener's girl?" Marie sang them beautifully; she would have been an ornament to any choir. But since Mother and I could not carry a tune, we let her sing alone.

As we got deeper into winter, we found ourselves coming closer and closer to two central areas: the hymnbook and the Bible. No matter how often we had been raided and plundered, Mother had managed to defend one object with more resolution than any other: the much-thumbed hymnal she had received for her confirmation shortly after the turn of the century. On the flyleaf, in Frau Liebe's beautiful hand, was the christening dedication: "Praise the Lord, O my soul, and be mindful of the blessings He hath bestowed upon thee," with the date, September 20, 1888. We had chosen that same day in September 1945 for Claudia's christening, and the same dedication. So with hymns we were on safe ground. If our memories could come up with only eleven or twelve of the fifteen verses of Paul Gerhardt's "Go forth my soul and seek delight," we could look up the others in the morning.

As Christmas Eve approached, we felt worried at first that melancholy would overwhelm us. But we set up a little fir tree and decorated it with stars that we wove from straw. With our iron ration of zlotys, I bought three pralines in Glowitz, so that each of us would have a present. And then Mother recited the Christmas story in the dark, the story she had read so many times on Christmas Eve. But never had the familiar story sounded quite as it did to me now:

> And it came to pass in those days, that there went out a decree from Caesar Augustus, that all the world should be taxed. (And this taxing was first made when Cyrenius

> was governor of Syria.) And all went to be taxed, every one into his own city. And Joseph also went up from Galilee, out of the city of Nazareth, into Judaea, unto the city of David, which is called Bethlehem (because he was of the house and lineage of David): To be taxed with Mary his espoused wife, being great with child. And so it was that, while they were there, the days were accomplished that she should be delivered. And she brought forth her firstborn son, and wrapped him in swaddling clothes, and laid him in a manger: because there was no room for them in the inn.

Wasn't that addressed directly and personally to us, in our fragile refuge in the gardener's cottage in Rumbske? Was there ever a more devout congregation?

> And there were in the same country shepherds abiding in the field, keeping watch over their flocks by night. And, lo, the angel of the Lord came upon them, and the glory of the Lord shone round about them: and they were sore afraid. And the angel said unto them, Fear not: for, behold, I bring you good tidings of great joy, which shall be unto all people. For unto you is born this day in the city of David a Savior, which is Christ the Lord. And this shall be a sign unto you; Ye shall find the babe wrapped in swaddling clothes and lying in a manger. And suddenly there was with the angel a multitude of the heavenly host praising God, and saying, Glory to God in the highest, and on earth peace, good will toward men.

The star of Bethlehem, a light shining in the darkness, in our darkness: fear not. We held hands for a long time in silence.

On New Year's Eve we went to bed early. What was there to wait up for? But of course we could not go to sleep. The longer I stayed awake, the more a certain thought took hold of me—not a gloomy one but a mixture of hope and gratitude: "I'm still here, I'm still alive! And if we've survived all of this, we can survive anything."

LIGHTS IN THE DARKNESS

As I lay there, a poem came to mind, a good-night poem in Low German by Theodor Storm, which none of us had brought up yet:

As all the streets fall still now,
The bells ring clear as they may.
Good night, your heart should sleep now,
And tomorrow's another day.

In the cradle lies your young one,
And I am with you too.
Of the sorrows of your life, none
Will be the end of you.

Once more let us be saying
Good evening and good night.
The moon o'er the rooftops is playing,
Our Lord keeps watch all night.

Journey to the West

The Emperor's Old Watch

A cold night in January, the sudden clumping of heavy boots; the door flew open, masked figures burst in. In the glow of their flashlights I saw pistols, glittering knives. I barely had time to grab the baby. Already tables and chairs were being knocked over, a plate crashed to the floor, they pushed us against the wall. Shouts of *"Uri! Uri!"*

"Nix *uri,* all gone, *uri* all gone!" I felt tempted to laugh bitterly right in the middle of this surge of fear and impotent rage. Where did they think we would get *uri* when previous marauders had cleaned us out? But Marie, panic-stricken, pushed into a corner by two bawling figures, blurted out, pointing toward the attic, "Up there, there's still one up there!"

Yes, in fact we did still have one watch, hidden in a corner of the attic, in a gap between two beams. Through all the raids and looting we had managed to hold on to it, until this January night in 1946: no ordinary jeweler's watch, no common or garden variety timepiece, but an antique gold pocket watch, a nineteenth-century masterpiece. One could even tell time in the dark with it; if you pushed a button, three bells would strike in succession. They told the hours, the quarters, and the minutes. I had inherited this watch from my Karzin grandfather, who had it from his father, Prussian secretary of state Robert von Puttkamer. He in turn had received it as a present from old Kaiser Wilhelm I; it had the imperial signature engraved on the cover. We knew it as "the emperor's old watch," as opposed to his "new clothes."

So now we lost that too. We heard its bells one more time; to me they sounded tearful, like a cry for help. For a moment silence fell amid all the din. And then the bandits, still bawling *"Uri!"* but this time in triumph, carried it off. My immediate reaction was to give Marie a resounding slap in the face, half in fury at the loss, half, or even more, in response to our helplessness. At that, of course, she really started to wail, in competition with the baby. I shouted at her, "Will you be quiet now!" Finally we began to tidy the devastated rooms, all together.

This episode finally brought to maturity a decision I had been mulling over: I would undertake a reconnaissance mission to the west, to see how things were and whether we could find a safe haven anywhere. After all, we knew nothing of conditions in "Germany" or "the Reich," nothing about the last days of the war or its aftermath west of the Oder and the Elbe. We had no idea how the British and Americans were administering their sectors and treating the population there.

I would come back, and if things were better there in the west, we would all set out as soon as summer weather made it a little safer for the baby and ourselves.

When I told Mother of my decision, she hesitated at first, understandably enough. Her thoughts were always with Father Jesko in Danzig. How was he faring, what would become of him? But in fact we could do nothing for him. If and when they would ever release him was written in the stars. And if they did release him, they might very well send him directly to the west. We had heard that the Poles took all those they wanted to be rid of and shipped them west in sealed railroad cars. And then the important thing would be to have a place for Father where he could be safe and recuperate.

Our cottage in Rumbske would never be a home; this last attack had proved that beyond any doubt. How much longer could we manage to survive here anyway? Marie's maxim remained as true as ever: "A person's got to eat." But her fleshpots were empty, and we could foresee the end of the sugar. Would we be able to get potatoes and flour in the future? There wasn't even anything to steal.

In the autumn, the fields of our old estate had been left fallow for the second year running; the spring now promised little activity. Without machinery and tractors, horses and livestock, seed and fertilizer, nothing could be done. In all likelihood, terrible shortages would occur, perhaps a famine of the sort we knew of from chronicles of the Thirty Years' War. *Vae victis!* The Germans would be the last to be given anything—and their children would be the first to die.

We had fewer and fewer items suitable for selling in an emergency, though at least we still had our fur coats. But they were our last reserves, which we needed to pay for our emigration.

Finally Mother assented, and I began to make my preparations. Curiously, in all our long deliberations, one thing we did not even consider: the risk associated with the journey, and the possibility that I might not be readmitted to the country. On this score Mother manifested unshakable confidence in me. In response to the fears aroused by my hikes to Stolp, or any of my other escapades, she would always reply curtly and firmly, "Libussa will be back." That indeed was what I promised her this time.

From Stolp to Stettin

The Russians never showed any interest in our furs; they considered them purely utilitarian objects, of which they themselves had plenty, and perhaps of much better quality than the Germans'. Mother had a beautiful mink, I a beaver. The mink had to be saved so that we could turn it into cash later; our new masters wanted to make a profit on shipping out the undesirable "natives." But now I took the beaver to Glowitz and sold it for a few hundred zlotys to the Polish mayor's wife, with whom I had stayed in touch, despite the debacle with the runner. My "war chest" was now reasonably full.

Otherwise the preparations did not take long. Two thousand reichsmarks were sewn into my much-patched old track suit. They came from the iron cash box that we had buried under the roots of an old oak in the park before we fled the estate. I filled my rucksack with bread, made this time with proper zloty-bought yeast and without the addition of ground birch bark, in the hope that it would keep. Not much else needed to be done, and on February 2, 1946, I set off into the unknown, a second Stanley off to look for David Livingstone in darkest Africa.

"Give me two months," I said as I took leave of Mother, "and don't worry. I'll be back by my birthday, April fifth, at the latest."

"Of course you will, child." Mother's impassive countenance was no doubt intended to give me, or both of us, courage.

Incidentally, a couple of days later, the Polish mayor turned up at the gardener's cottage to ask Mother where I was. News of my departure had of course spread through the village like wildfire.

"She's gone to the West. She wants to see how things are there. And then she'll come back and get us."

"To Germany?" The man was amazed. He laughed. "You no see her again! Leave, yes, but no come back. Never. Impossible, absolutely prohibited, border strictly guarded! Want to bet?"

"Why not? Mayor, you will lose. Within two months. The only thing is, I'm afraid I have nothing to wager."

Another peal of laughter. "Never mind, never mind, is

done! If daughter beat Poland, then I come celebrate with chicken!"

I spent the first night with Grandmother in Karzin. She quickly wrote letters to her son and two daughters in the West. She had no envelopes, but those I could get when I reached my destination. Very early the next morning I went on to Stolp and made for the office I had visited months earlier with Hannah Brandt. That office no longer existed, and I was directed to another building, to a Polish government agency and a door there with a sign saying "Emigration" in German.

Behind the door, sitting at a desk with the red-and-white Polish flag, was an impeccable uniform, as new and freshly pressed as the face above it. Not a hint of a Polish accent. What change of circumstances, what personal history, lay behind that facade?

"Good morning. Have a seat, please. You wish to leave Pomorze?"

"Yes. I mean . . ." What could I say; did it have anything to do with wishing?

"Do you have any papers on you, any form of identification?"

All I had was my certificate from the typhoid vaccination the previous summer, which did not even have my name on it. But evidently that was sufficient. Probably the only thing that mattered was getting people out; my name, maiden name, date and place of birth were noted down, the last item in its new Polonized form, Rumsko for Rumbske. The man took it all on faith. Or had he heard of me; did he know me somehow? He looked at me long and quizzically. Then an inscrutable smile.

"Would you sign here, please. And again here. Everything must be done properly, you understand? I shall read you what you've signed: 'I am leaving Poland for Germany of my own free will and irrevocably. I know that I am not allowed to return, and that to attempt to do so constitutes a criminal offense.' All right?"

I nodded silently.

"Excellent. And now one hundred fifty zlotys, please. Thank you. Here is your exit permit. And now to the station." A glance at his watch, another smile. "Your train leaves at ten-fourteen, correct? You must hurry. A pleasant journey." And at no additional charge, a curt Prussian suggestion of a bow.

So after just a few minutes I was back on the street, stamped permit in hand, and thoroughly perplexed: could it really be so simple? Might the reports of plundering and harassment be nothing but rumors, malicious inventions? Ten-fourteen—that was the same time the train left in peacetime. First, second, and third class, and a dining car. Arrival in Stettin at two in the afternoon, arrival in Berlin, Stettin Station, at three-eighteen. Our train: you could catch it in Stolp in the morning and be in Berlin by midafternoon, in plenty of time for an evening rendezvous.

Bahnhofstrasse, with facades in both the imposing, heavy-looking late-nineteenth-century style and graceful art nouveau. There was Aunt Melanie's balcony, where I had slept the previous summer. On the right, at the very end of the street, the station hotel. When returning from the big world, we would sometimes spend the night there, because the last local train would have left hours earlier. Depart Berlin, Stettin Station, at four in the afternoon on the dot, arrive in Stolp at nine twenty-four in the evening. Last stop.

"Halt! Papers!" The militia were everywhere, sealing off the station. It was swarming with them, as though the military had been put on red alert or a general mobilization had just begun. I showed my newly acquired form. "Buy ticket!" The tone became more gruff. I was led to the counter: another one hundred fifty zlotys to pay; half my money was already spent. They did not give me an actual ticket. Then on down the platform, escorted on either side like a dangerous criminal waiting to make a break for it.

Sure enough, the train was there already. But it still had no locomotive. Nor did it look quite the way trains did in peacetime. It had a rather odd makeup: in front, passenger carriages with the windows boarded up, in back, cattle cars. And a sinister contrast: a colorful bustle outside the passenger carriages, with much coming and going, shouting, noise, and laughter. A deathly hush at the rear, which was where they were leading me. The Polish and the German sections of the train. A door to one of the cattle cars was pulled open: "Get in!" The door banged shut. The darkness hit me like a blow.

When my eyes had become accustomed to it, and I could see in the dim light that entered through chinks and cracks, I realized that the wagon was full of people, forty or fifty women, children, and old people. Women especially, young and old. Baggage everywhere: suitcases, a couple of crates, cardboard boxes, and bundles. Presumably all these people meant to leave their homes forever; and they had brought with them anything they still had left that could be carried. In the middle of the car, the baggage had been piled up in a mound. No one had enough space to lie down. Only to sit, with knees drawn up. I picked my way over legs and suitcases toward the wall, instinct telling me to get as far away as possible from the entrance and to take refuge in a dark corner with my back protected. The people next to me mumbled and grumbled at having to squeeze closer together, but finally I managed to slip in among them.

We waited for something to happen, for the train to give a jerk and move off. Stolp in East Pomerania, our proud "little Paris." Whenever I heard the phrase as a child, I would wonder, why "little"? Compared to Rumbske the town seemed enormous. Real trams ran in the streets, and Zeeck's department store had an elevator. Then, during the war, we actually saw a special train for the armed forces on leave marked "Stolp–Paris," as though those were the two poles of our world.

The date was February 3, 1946. Comparatively mild for this time of year, the temperature around freezing or a little above. A silly phrase ran through my head: "Better warm and steamy than cold and clear." How true. At least our being jammed together had the advantage of producing body heat; we were almost sweating.

An hour passed, then another, perhaps a third. Because no one had a watch, we had no way of measuring time. But we were so impatient, so nervous about what lay ahead, that time seemed to crawl.

To while away the time and divert myself, I thought of rhymes and sayings:

We journey all on the same old train
Through time on our spinning star.
We look outside. It's too much pain.
We journey all on the same old train.
And no one knows how far.

Erich Kästner again. His books were banned and burned during the years when Bahnhofstrasse in Stolp was known as Adolf-Hitler-Strasse, but still people secretly passed them around, read them and loved them. I poked around in my memory, recited to myself the bitter refrain from the "Masked Ball in the Mountains," which he wrote in 1930: "If only we had won the war/How lucky that we didn't."

Suddenly a huge jolt, a moment of panic, then relief: the locomotive had arrived. The whistle blew and blew, probably to call together all the passengers for the front part of the train. And then, at long last, the train slowly began to move. There should have been a band to see us off, playing the old journeyman's song "Must I then / must I then / leave my village so dear . . ." My winter training was paying off: verses flooded into my brain—Freiligrath's "Emigrants' Song," which begins:

I cannot take my eyes from you,
I have to watch whate'er you do.
You pass your bags with troubled brow
And trembling hands up to the crew.

The freight cars rattled and banged and shook us through and through. No smoothly gliding express with deep cushioned seats this time. But all that mattered was that we were moving.

The familiar stations, first Schlawe, then Köslin, then Belgard. At each stop, light burst into our darkness as a few more people were shoved into our already overcrowded car. But perhaps this time we would get as far as Stargard. I took out my bread and munched contentedly, asking myself again where those appalling rumors about the terrors of emigration had come from. People must have made them up; after all, if no one was allowed to return, how could there be any eyewitness accounts?

By now night had fallen, still very early. Somewhere in the middle of nowhere the train slowed to a walking pace. The locomotive tooted signals, as if asking for permission to proceed, or being self-important: "Look out! Here I come!" Then the train stopped.

A shot rang out, very close and very loud, the signal for loud shouts. The door was ripped open—cries of terror, lanterns flickering, a horde surging in: wild figures dimly glimpsed amid the chaos and the confusion, men, but also youths and women, savage women, perhaps the worst of all, screaming, slavering, striking, snatching. More pistol shots, right over our heads, booming like cannon in the small space, numbness, knives and axes, fists, kicks, feet trampling over bodies, and always this bellowing, and cries of fear and pain. Suitcases and crates, boxes and bundles, sprouted wings, flew up in the air and out the door. The horde followed them out, and the door banged shut.

Darkness and silence. From very far away, the locomotive tooted its signal, the train jolted and rumbled off as though nothing had happened. An objective observer of the scene, stopwatch in hand, would probably have shaken his head: what to the victims seemed like never-ending hellish torment was actually over in a flash. Three or four minutes, perhaps, five at most.

Spasmodic gasps, but only very little soft sobbing. Someone vomited. A child's voice: "Mama, Mama, where are you?" And an old man, like a child again, and as though his whole world depended on it, repeated over and over, "My watercolors, my watercolors . . ."

I had come through the attack relatively unscathed. With

my rucksack on my back and my back pressed against the wall and my feet braced on the floor, my hands in front of my body for protection, nothing had happened to me. Besides, the attackers wanted the hand luggage, and I had none. But the hope that the danger might be past proved sorely mistaken. This was only the beginning. New raids followed, and they turned out to be far worse.

To begin with, a wave of dread now preceded them. When the locomotive whistled and the train braked and came to a halt, my heart beat like a hammer, my breath became shallow and forced, my whole body tensed. I noticed that my teeth were chattering uncontrollably.

Sometimes there were false alarms. The locomotive would whistle, the train would brake and stop—and we would pull into a station. Then it was the militiamen who opened the doors and shone their flashlights around the car. Although they must know the answer, they asked, "Were you attacked?" "Yes, yes, attacked." People replied timidly, piteously, hoping for protection. But the only response was derisive laughter, and the door banged shut again.

And then the attacks were no longer aimed at the luggage, because there was none left, but at the people themselves. Jackets, coats, and dresses were stripped off, bodies greedily patted for money or jewels, anything of value. In the second attack I lost my rucksack with the bread in it, in the third the rest of my zlotys, and in the fourth my boots. They had served me well for almost a year, beginning with the first day of our trek, on all those hikes to Stolp, on all my forays.

Stargard at last, and a longer stopover. No more rhymes occurred to me now, only bitter thoughts: the whole thing seemed organized, done according to plan, with the full knowledge of the militia and the railwaymen in cahoots with the leaders of the marauding bands. Why else would the train slow just in time for the ambush? And if the authorities wanted to prevent these raids, which they clearly knew about, they could put an armed guard on the train. No, this was neither chance nor powerlessness to help; it was part of a calculated and deliberate policy.

More thoughts, and questions silently directed to the front part of the train: how did the people there feel about these scenes of terror and destruction? Did they say to themselves, It's the Germans' turn now? Did they think, Serves them right? Or did some of them at least feel stirrings of pity, revulsion, and shame?

It is a fundamental error to project our gentle souls, our good-natured ways, and our idealism onto alien peoples. . . . Only to members of our own race do we owe honesty, decency, comradeship, and loyalty, to no one else. How the Russians or the Czechs fare leaves me totally indifferent. Whatever these other peoples possess in the way of good racial stock, we will get for ourselves, if need be by stealing their children and bringing them up among us. Whether other races are living in comfort or dropping from starvation interests me only insofar as we need them as slaves for our own culture, otherwise it is of no interest to me. If ten thousand Russian women collapse from weakness while digging antitank trenches, the only thing of interest to me is whether the trenches get dug for Germany. Certainly we will never be heartless or vicious when it is not necessary. We Germans, the only people in the world with a decent attitude toward animals, will adopt a decent attitude toward these human animals too, but it is a crime against our race to worry about them and to attribute our own ideals to them. . . .

I also want to speak to you openly about a very difficult topic. It can be discussed openly here among us, yet we shall never mention it in public. . . . I am referring to the evacuation of the Jews, the extermination of the Jewish people. It is one of those things that pass easily over the lips. "The Jewish people will be exterminated," says every Party member, "of course, it's on our agenda, exclusion of the Jews, extermination: will do." But then they all come forward, our eighty million good Germans, and each of them has his own example of a decent Jew. Right, of course, the rest are all animals, but this one here is a fine Jew. But of those who talk like that, none has looked on and stood by.

Most of you know what it is like to see a hundred corpses lying in a heap, or five hundred, or a thousand. To have been through that and—except for a few examples of human weakness—remained decent has made us strong. This is a glorious page of our history, which never has been and never will be written.[15]

We journeyed on. After Stargard there were no more attacks. In any case, there was probably nothing left to make them worthwhile. After a time, the train's slowing down to a walk and dull thudding announced something other than violence: the railway bridge over the Oder. And shortly afterward, in the middle of the night, we reached Stettin.

Nightmare in Scheune

Had we left Polish territory behind us now, had we been released into "the Reich," into Germany? That hope quickly turned out to be illusory. No German train was waiting on another platform, no locomotive from the Reich railway came puffing up to take our cars in tow. The front and rear parts of the train were uncoupled. But no one opened the doors for us. We could only hear and glimpse through the cracks in the car guards moving up and down outside. Another long and fearful wait began. Later we were shunted back and forth, this way and that, almost indecisively, it seemed to us, as though they did not know what to do with these cars and their pathetic human freight. And then we were leaving the station and heading out of Stettin.

Finally the train stopped, the doors slid open, flashlight beams zigzagged over us, we blinked in the light. "Out! Everybody out! Move along!" We struggled to our feet, legs stiff, our whole bodies aching. Slowly this crowd of pitiful figures—old men, women, and children—trickled out onto the platform. All around, militia with submachine guns. "Faster! Faster! Line up in twos!" Why all the shouting, yelling, and brutality in such situations? What was this supposed to achieve or forestall? Where did they ever find such an assortment of wild, twisted, evil, brutal faces?

A driving snowstorm had set in; we shivered in the biting wind. With militiamen circling constantly, the column of some four hundred people set off. I sensed a building nearby. "Scheune—the sugar factory," whispered someone who apparently knew the area. And still the blows with rifle butts, the incessant yelling, most of it in Polish and incomprehensible to us. But the girl walking beside me understood. "Letters," she whispered. "No letters. Anyone caught with letters will be punished—as a spy." I tore up those letters my grandmother had given me and dropped the scraps into a hedge we were passing.

Walls now, and the buildings. Our column wound to the right and to the left, turned corners, scrambled over rubble, went up and down stairs, as though it was a matter of destroying our sense of direction, which we did not have in any case.

At last a door: "In here! Move!" The door was locked behind us. We groped around, looking for a wall to lean against, a place to sit a little out of the way, if possible, so that we would not get stepped on. Eventually our weary eyes began to function again. Through high windows with broken panes a hint of early light came in, along with a flurry of snow. We could make out a very large, completely bare hall. Much too large to be heated by the warmth of four hundred bodies; if you lay down on the concrete floor and tried to sleep, the cold soon woke you and forced you to get up and move around. For bodily functions they had placed a couple of buckets in a corner. But they were already overflowing—God knows when they had last been emptied. That part of the room gave off an infernal stench.

We waited and waited. Nothing happened. A child whimpered for bread that no one had to give. Otherwise it was very still, just here and there a little whispering. As the hours crawled by at a snail's pace, we dozed, dropped off, woke up abruptly. The daylight crept away as it had come, in a prolonged twilight.

The girl who had walked beside me in the column had

stayed with me ever since. I told her, "When it gets dark, they'll move us again. Let's get close to the door so we're the first ones out."

"No, no, anything but that! Who knows what they'll do to us."

"It'll be far worse if we wait and wait and then hear from the others how terrible it was. Better to get it over with quickly." The girl trembled; I put my arm around her and coaxed her toward the door.

I was right: they must have needed darkness for whatever they had in mind. The door crashed open, the usual blinding light, the usual bellowing: "Line up in pairs! Move!" I took the girl's hand. Another labyrinthine route: the yard, corners, corridors, stairs, with militia everywhere, dealing out blows with their rifle butts as though driving cattle to the slaughter. At last we found ourselves in a large hall half-lit by candles. Behind a long table sat the uniformed lord of the occasion. He had a book in front of him. And piles of jewelry and money, presumably left by others who were rushed through here before us.

"Strip! Quick! Over there!" A kind of screen had been placed along the wall. But it was at such an angle that the man at the desk could see us perfectly. We had to undress, not down to our underwear but completely, and throw all our clothes to two men, who took knives out of their boots and went to work with practiced moves: everything was slit open, no seam was spared. The last of my money came to light and landed on the table, two thousand marks that had survived the attacks of the bandits between Belgard and Stargard. Then our clothes were tossed in a heap of rags, probably also left by our predecessors.

"Quick! Get dressed! Quick! Quick!" I grabbed whatever came to hand: some underwear, my track suit, or what was left of it, a bit of string to hold up the pants. And even a pair of shoes, coming apart and too big for me, but still better than going barefoot on the long roads that might lie ahead.

Now the book: "Sign here that money and valuables were lawfully deposited!"

Lawfully! But who would ever check our names and identities? I wrote down the first name that popped into my head: "Mathilde Gomorrah," and I tried to make it as legible as I could. As the law required.

But what help were all my good intentions against the temptation of the moment? The man at the table was staring with interest at the next two women taking off their clothes. I quickly snatched two fifty-mark notes from the pile.

"Move!" Another gauntlet to run, more bellowing, more blows—and what seemed like an interminable walk. Sometimes we were stopped, and they raked us with lights, up and down our bodies. Dark figures were hanging around everywhere, staring at us, sizing us up. We found ourselves in another dark space, the only clue to whose size was the echo of the door as it slammed.

"Did you see those men?" the girl whispered. "The way they were looking us over? I'll bet they already have us picked out—"

"Hush!" I groped my way along the wall: was there any way out? I felt a window opening, not so high in the wall as the one in the hall where we had spent the day; it couldn't be that difficult to haul myself up to it. "Here, we can get out here. We'll give it a try. There's bound to be some place to hide out there!"

"No, no, no!" She was trembling again and sobbing. No amount of persuasion helped. All she could say was "No, no!" She was paralyzed by fear, fatigue perhaps, a loss of the will to do anything on her own behalf. Besides, there was certainly a risk: how high up was this hall; hadn't we gone up stairs to get to it? How far was the drop to the ground? Did the window give on a closed courtyard? Might there be a guard standing below?

I had to make the attempt on my own. The hall of a sugar factory out in the country could not be that high off the ground. I pulled myself up to the window and listened for two or three minutes; in this cold, any guard would have to keep moving to stay warm. I heard nothing, but then I could not see anything, either. I lowered myself cautiously from the sill and let go.

A drop, not a fall: in fact, the hall was almost level with the ground outside. No one shouted "Who goes there?" No flashlight beam swept over me. I groped my way forward, in the opposite direction from the shouts of "Move! Move!" and the screams. A bit of stone wall, a hedge, then out in the open. In the light reflected off the snow, strange shadows loomed, two or three prehistoric monsters. They were tanks that had met their end here, whether German or Russian I could not tell. Nor did I care.

I had never had any dealings with tanks, but the newsreel reportages on victories in Poland, France, Africa, and Russia had stuck in my mind: you had to scramble up and get inside at the top through a hatch with a cover. What the pictures had promised proved correct. The least badly damaged of the monsters became my refuge. It even had a seat in it. With a sigh of relief, I settled into it. No one would ever look for me here.

One thing the newsreels had forgotten to mention: it was freezing inside those steel tombs. The cold pierced straight through my scanty clothing and even drove away my ravenous hunger. If only that girl had come with me, so we could have kept each other warm! Soon I was chilled to the bone. "You'll catch your death of cold, child," was what we would have said earlier if someone had gone out so inadequately dressed. Only the screams that reached me from time to time—far away, but clear enough—only those screams told me that I had chosen the lesser evil.

When dawn came, I peered through a jagged hole in the side of the tank, then through the observation slits, and finally out the hatch. The crosses on the sides informed me that these tanks were German. Incidentally, in the newsreels they never showed German tanks as wrecks; we only saw the other side's. After a time, people came into view—our original column, not very far from where I was hidden. They marched toward the railroad yard, guarded by only two militiamen, who walked at the head of the procession. I clambered out of my tank and crept toward them, running bent double in the shelter of the hedge. Just before the ramp along the tracks, I caught up with them and slipped into the line.

Was there ever such a wretched collection of people? All that remained to remind one of proper clothing was rags and tatters. Their hair hung in tangles, their faces were pale and hollow with exhaustion, when they were not bloodied or bruised. One woman wore only a shirt and held a completely naked infant in her arms. I saw my former companion. She was squatting on the ground, hugging her knees, her upper body rocking back and forth. Spasms of hysterical sobbing shook her, without her being able to cry. It was impossible to speak to her.

All a Human Being Needs

"A train, a train!" Everyone jumped up. And there it was, steaming toward us out of the gloom. It gradually took on contours, it braked, it came to a stop directly in front of us on the platform. No cattle cars this time, but a real passenger train, even if most of the windows were covered with boards or cardboard.

A man got out—no, an official, a conductor of the old school from the Reich Railways: proper uniform, cap at the right angle, ticket pouch slung across his chest, clean boots. He got off—and raised both hands above his head, like a man surrendering. For he could probably guess what was coming, dreaded a sudden surge, knew four hundred people were there, all wanting to touch him, embrace him, kiss him; he made this trip every day or every other day. "All right, it's all right, everything's going to be all right," he called out soothingly, like a father to a horde of lost children. And "Climb aboard, please, all aboard, we're leaving soon, going home."

Home, really? people asked in embarrassment. They hesitated. "But we can't . . . we have no money left; how are we going to pay for the tickets?" It was bizarre, crazy really: rulers and Reich came and went, whole worlds collapsed, the sky fell in, yet this German love of order remained intact. No sooner did we meet an official than it reasserted itself, as was only proper. Was it Lenin who once said that if the Germans had a revolution and needed to storm a railway station, they would all go and buy platform tickets first? In 1918, when it was reported to the king of Saxony that a revolution was in progress, and people carrying red flags were marching on his palace, he cried incredulously, "But is that allowed?"

The conductor laughed and let us have a glimpse of his white hair. He took off his cap, absolutely against regulations, and, to soften his authority, waved it about, acting the fairground barker: "Special, special, ladies and gentlemen, free ride! All aboard, please, for the special free ride . . ." That worked. We scrambled aboard the train, stroked the seats in amazement. The luggage nets were quite superfluous. And as soon as the locomotive had been shunted to the other end of the train, we were off. Suddenly time seemed to fly, even though the train was creeping along. In no time at all, we were in Angermünde.

The train ride ended here, and so did the feeling of being looked after, almost as by a father. No one came to meet us or counsel us. No station mission, no Red Cross serving coffee or hot soup. A train to Berlin? Yes, later on, maybe . . . The sense of solidarity among these four hundred people dissolved as quickly as it had formed.

The waiting room was intact, though devoid of furniture. Only the built-in bar recalled better days. I lay down on the floor behind it. Weakness swept over me, compounded of fatigue, gnawing hunger, tension, and now the sudden absence of tension. I thought, or rather, my whole body suddenly gave up and said: No more, just let me lie here, lie here and perhaps die. Never get up again, never.

A jab in the ribs. With effort I opened my eyes. I saw a Russian towering over me, tall and broad-shouldered. He had kicked me to see if I was still alive. He looked at me, I looked back at him, and he said, "You, woman, hungry?"

Hungry was putting it mildly. It had been two full days since I last had anything to eat, and that had not been much, because I had wanted to stretch my rations. Now I was too weak to reply.

But this Russian understood me without words. From his trousers pocket he pulled a hunk of bread and handed it down to me. Clean it was not: there were bits of pocket fluff clinging to it, and God knows what else besides. But that did not trouble me in the least. I sat up, took the bread, and began to chew. I could hardly remember when anything had tasted so delicious. For a while the Russian stood there watching me. Then he nodded and left.

When it comes right down to it, what does a human being need? Just a piece of bread—and someone who understands, who is in the right place at the right time, who looks at one and asks, "You, woman, hungry?"

My weakness had vanished. And wonder of wonders, a train to Berlin was being coupled together. I bought a ticket, as one is supposed to do, and got on that train.

"Another of Them Poor War Victims"

I knew my way around Berlin. I had spent many years there, first as a schoolgirl at the Königin-Luise-Stift, while my brothers attended the Arndt Gymnasium in Dahlem. Later on, during the war, I had worked for the Foreign Ministry, monitoring BBC news broadcasts.

My thoughts automatically returned to the events of those years. That sensational rumor that made the rounds one night, which no one quite believed or dared to report officially: the news that Rudolf Hess, the Führer's deputy, had landed in England. In no time the Berliners had made up a satirical verse about it:

For years they've trumpeted through the land:
"Just watch us descend on Engeland!"

But when a fellow goes and lands his plane,
They promptly declare that he's insane.

I had last seen the city in autumn 1944. By that time many buildings were already in ruins. But a lifetime, a century, seemed to have passed since then. How was one supposed to find one's way around? There was nothing I could orient myself by in this wasteland, where an occasional stovepipe poked out of the ground, testifying to the existence of cave dwellers below. I had to keep asking for directions, an exhausting process. But the Berliners' caustic humor remained intact: The Biedermanns lived on Stubenrauchplatz—that is, they did if the building was still standing and its inhabitants were still alive. When I asked how to get there, a Berliner replied, "You want to get to Steglitz, Fräulein? Stubenrauchplatz? Sorry, can't help you. Isn't that behind the moon? And shouldn't that be Stubbenrauch, with two *b*'s, like 'rubble'? Plenty of that around--just have to keep your eyes peeled."

Worn out from the long hike, I arrived just as the last light was fading. And there it was: the house was still standing, the plate on the door read "A. Biedermann." And Aunt Deten answered my knock.

The Biedermanns were more than surprised to see me; in fact, they were somewhat appalled, probably at the way I looked but also at the prospect that I might become a burden on them. They had had to give up all but one room in their apartment, and they had very little to eat. I assured them that I would be moving on the next morning. They gave me some barley soup, and I slept rolled up in a blanket on the bedside rug.

My next destination was in Zehlendorf. That was where Ilse Hagens lived, an old and dear friend of my mother's. Perhaps being halfway rested helped, or perhaps the destruction in the southwestern part of the city was not so bad; in any case, my memory began to serve me again, and I found my way without any trouble. No. 12 Malinowskistrasse: luckily that house, too, was still standing. As though everything were the same as ever, Gretchen answered my ring. Gretchen Voigt, like our Marie a familiar figure. For as long as we could remember, she had been Ilse Hagens's cook, chambermaid, housekeeper, and confidante rolled into one—one of those "pearls" who used to devote their lives to the service of a single family, often taking care of several generations, until they imperceptibly became part of the family, with which they identified completely.

"Hello, I—" The door slammed in my face and cut me off in midsentence.

I rang again, a little more insistently. Gretchen appeared again, looking even more unfriendly, and silently held out a fifty-pfennig piece. "No, no, I want to speak to Frau von Hagens, please!"

An upstairs window opened, and Aunt Ilse looked out: "Who are you, and what do you want?"

"To see you, Aunt Ilse, I'm Libussa from Rumbske!"

"It's not possible! My God, is it really you? You look a sight!"

Once inside, and looking at myself in a mirror for the first time in days, I could only echo her exclamation. Filthy, with tangled hair and a black eye, my clothes reduced to rags—I would have made a perfect model of a beggar girl for students at an art school.

The luxury of being able to wash, to eat at a table with a tablecloth, off china plates and with silver cutlery, to have a sofa to sleep on, and warm covers! Gretchen overwhelmed me with solicitude, doubtless trying to compensate for the unfortunate scene at the door. But now, perhaps as a delayed aftereffect of my night in the tank, or because I could let myself go here, for the first time in a year I got really sick, with a high fever and alternating bouts of burning up and shivering. It was a week before I could respond to what people said to me. Then I told my tales of Pomerania, and in return heard a little about conditions in Germany, about the occupying powers and their zones, the role of the Allies in Berlin. And the Potsdam Agreement, which stipulated that the German population had to be moved out of the areas east of the Oder and the Neisse in "an orderly and humane fashion." Perhaps I should forget about the role as beggar girl and instead offer myself as an exemplar of the orderliness and humanity with which this agreement was being implemented.

After ten days I still did not feel very steady on my legs, but my energy was returning, and along with it, impatience. I had already lost precious time, and I had to move on. Gretchen had patched up my track suit as best she could. And to guard against my catching cold again, they gave me a snow-white silk scarf, once a splendid accessory for a man's dress suit. Its immaculate elegance made an interesting contrast with the rest of my getup. I also received good advice from people who had had some experience of traveling between Berlin and the western zones.

Trains were running, at least almost to the border of the Russian zone. They might be shabby, slow, and crushingly full, with people even spilling onto the steps, but I did not mind that, and the crowding even had an advantage: officials checking for passports or travel permits would be unlikely to nab me. With streams of people winding their way through the country, the possibility of imposing effective control seemed limited in any case, in stark contrast to the mania for checking up on everything, to the orders and especially the prohibitions, with which the rulers of the Thousand-Year Reich had kept people in line to the very end—indeed, especially at the very end. Chaos has its benefits.

Wild rumors were circulating before we got to the border: the Russians were said to lie in wait like hunters, ready to bag refugees attempting to cross into the West. But there were entrepreneurs who promised to escort you safely across in return for a carton of cigarettes, a large sum of money, or other valuables. I had nothing to give, and besides, I recalled from the hunts of my youth and my later forays to Karzin and Stolp, the more people you have together, the more noise they make. This would be even more true of groups heavily laden with baggage and stumbling along blindly behind a leader who would be sure to abandon them at the first sign of trouble.

So I set off on my own and found my way without incident to the British sector, marked by jeeps patrolling with their headlights on. In the light of morning I came upon a road. With the sun rising, it was not difficult to tell which way was west. After a while a truck came along. I waved, and it stopped. The driver let me get in. He was an older man, heavyset and easygoing, happy simply to have me talk to him and keep him awake. He was going as far as Hanover.

From talking to him, I picked up some new concepts—that of the "hitchhiker," for instance. And sure enough, just after we had discussed this phenomenon, we saw one: a ragged-looking man with a small child. My driver had no intention of stopping; he found my stories sufficiently entertaining. But I appealed to his paternal instincts: "Look at that poor child in his skimpy little coat!" The weather was cold and rainy; patches of snow lay everywhere. The driver grumbled but pulled over. The man picked up his child and ran after us—and then baffled and touched me by bowing elegantly and kissing my hand. With wonderfully rolling Baltic intonation, he introduced himself: "Keyserling, at your service." How should one respond with suitable dignity to something so thoroughly unexpected? And it did not help one to remain dignified when one's memory promptly came up with the irreverent little couplet:

When God was done with everything,
He created last—Count Keyserling!

Perhaps, for future reference, someone should compile a guide to good manners after the apocalypse.

Everything continued to go like clockwork. Hanover was incredibly crowded, but I promptly located a train to Hamburg. On the train I found someone who gave me precise instructions for taking the municipal railway to the other station, from which trains departed for Neumünster and Kiel.

Two men were sitting across from me on the municipal

railway. As I looked out the window, one of them whispered to his chum, in broad Berlin dialect, loud enough for me to hear, "Look, another of them poor war victims!" I had to laugh: denizens of the Spree here, in Hamburg on the Alster. I realized that I had actually come through, that for the moment I could take a break from adventures. But only Berliners should be hired as commentators on the worst of times.

I thought of a story Mother liked to tell sometimes, from the period after the lost war, the first lost war of this glorious century—the time of the inflation, with its scandals and profiteers. During the Berlin Agricultural Exhibition, a gala reception took place for high society, with the gentlemen in tails, the ladies in evening dresses. Around midnight, a group of them decided to go over and watch the six-day bicycle races. And as they were led into their box, a working-class Berlin voice was heard from the cheap seats above them: "Just you take a look at that: there goes a flock of thirty-year jail sentences!" How did that go again? "After a lost war, comedies should be performed." And with all the seriousness due true comedy.

Journey to Pomerania

The Sweet Scent of Freedom

What luxury, what reveling in the joys of civilization, to soak in a hot bath, to have set before me a jug of hot milk and a plate of bread, cold cuts and eggs, with the quite superfluous injunction to "Eat up!" Troops back from the front must have felt as I did when they had three precious weeks full of opportunities for pleasure, wonder, and gratitude for what was still available.

For me the greatest joy was to be reunited with my brother. How happy Mother would be when she heard that the war, which had swallowed up two of her sons, had spared the third and last of them. He was here, at the rendezvous spot we had prudently arranged ahead of time. The Allies had released him soon after the surrender. Rather than dwelling on what was lost and gone, he had already begun making plans for a fresh start, for finishing secondary school and going to the university, for his future.

And for three weeks I kept finding new things to be amazed by. The way people moaned and groaned! This estate in Holstein, just inland from the Baltic coast, was of course crammed with people, just like every other house, every tiny room, and every broken-down shed in the entire country. So the property owners were complaining about the propertyless, the natives about the refugees, who were allegedly taking everything. And for their part, the refugees were complaining about the lack of sympathy, the coldness, greed, and arrogance of the natives.

People who had to get by on "average consumer's rations," who did not live in the country or do farming, and who did not have "vitamin C"—connections with farmers, bakers, officials—were forced to go on arduous expeditions to obtain food, exchanging what they had left, or playing dangerous games in attempting to get things on the black market. The currency hardly had any value anymore; the real currency was named Chesterfield, or Lucky Strike.

And then I heard people saying, Oh, look at the occupying powers, the British, or the Americans, requisitioning housing just like that, insisting on the German uniforms being dyed, and, as if that weren't enough, handing out questionnaires on everyone's past political posture and affiliations!

"I ask you, my dear, what did we know, what could we do about it? Actually, I was always opposed; wherever it was safe, I would say 'Good morning' instead of 'Heil Hitler.' But what choice did you have but to go along with it? No, honestly, these foreigners haven't a clue!"

On the promenade, the poetically inclined nature-lover will meet acquaintances who will buttonhole him and, in spite of fields and forests and meadows all around, will involve him in conversations altogether inappropriate to nature, and before he knows it, the dialogue will turn into a monologue, an impassioned political plea. "It's true I divorced my Jewish wife," one party explains to him, "but it was inevitable that we would break up—it would have happened in normal times too. Dictatorships don't have a monopoly on unhappy marriages. Besides, I sent her money as long as it was possible." The man stands there among high trees, as though they were the High Court. Unasked, he defends himself. He is practicing. He is polishing up his alibi. He is trying to line up people on whom he can test the force of his arguments.

The trees and the friend he meets out walking have no choice but to listen to him. He demands that he be acquitted. Then he goes on his way. Fear and a guilty conscience run after him.

The next fellow to come along assures one that although he was wearing the Party badge until very recently, he was never actually in the Party. "I was only a candidate for admission," he says. "I never became a member, although it would have simplified many things for me. If you only knew what I did to stay out of the Party! God knows, it wasn't easy not to be drawn in." We are standing on a road that runs between fields. In the farmyard over yonder, a cock crows. . . .

The third, another fleeting acquaintance, proves even more eager to confide. He opens not only his heart but also, figuratively speaking, his fly. In spite of the Nuremberg Laws, he slept from time to time with a Jewish girl, and now he is taking soundings on whether these pleasures, punishable at the time, create the proper political impression. After all, he made common cause with a Jewess at a time when it was forbidden! Doesn't that mean that he was active as an enemy of the state, if only in a horizontal position? Might not his sinful past, he wonders, be of use to him in the future? He tries to read in my face how I assess his case and his prospects. The fact that I think he's a pig doesn't bother him.

The paths through woods and fields resemble corridors in an imaginary courthouse. Those who have received summonses, more or less petty scoundrels, pace nervously, waiting for the bailiff to summon them, and draw every passerby into conversation. "It might help," they think. "You never know."[16]

Terrible conditions, no end of complaining. Perhaps everything was relative. But did people realize how much they still had, or had managed to recover? That here in the West, at least, the end of the war meant the beginning of peace and opportunity, a liberation, because despotism and force had been swept away, like the terrors of winter by the warm winds of spring? Did they smell the sweet scent of freedom, now that instead of the Führer's orders and the commands of marauding bandits dependable rules had been instituted? "Righteousness exalteth a nation," it says in the Bible, "but sin is a reproach to any people."

Meanwhile I had been receiving advice from all sides, all of it unsolicited, and all with the same thrust: "Stay here, don't go back there, there's no point, it can't be done, you're bound to be arrested and sent to prison camp, maybe even to Siberia." I had no one here to tell me, as Mother always had, "You can do it, I know you can." It weighed on me, but there was no help for it. I had to go back; Mother, Marie, and the baby were waiting for me. I needed no advice on this score, still less all those grim warnings from people who thought they knew better.

Since I was not to be deterred from my ill-starred mission, I was at least given some useful things to take with me: a pair of ski pants and a windbreaker from prewar days, sturdy shoes, and a rucksack full of nourishing provisions. And an important document, crucial for these times and this occupation zone: an immigration permit for my family and Marie. The owners of the estate in Holstein signed an affidavit guaranteeing us a room.

Sleeping Beauty in Angermünde

The first leg of my return journey took me to a village near Braunschweig, close to the border of the Russian zone. Chance, or whatever other factor may have been at work, gave me the address. This was where my cousin Otti von Veltheim was living now, with her mother, Dorothea, known as Aunt Dolly. They were the granddaughter and daughter of Great-Uncle Gerhard and Great-Aunt Lena, the old Glowitzers.

Otti and Aunt Dolly had been taken in by relatives, but in the style of the times: they were quartered in a half-converted attic, reached by a rickety staircase. Of course we had a great deal to tell each other. When I arrived, Otti was not home; she was off somewhere, engaged in a chief occupation of the new era—smuggling between the zones, going east with American cigarettes, coming back with nylon stockings from Chemnitz or whatever else she could find. But they expected her back soon; in fact, later in the evening. And sure enough, the moment I climbed into her bed, she turned up.

Aunt Dolly brewed a fresh pot of coffee, and we started all over again. But the story took a surprising turn; when I got to the christening, and Great-Uncle Gerhard's name cropped up again, Otti suddenly stood up and declared, "You're not going alone; I'm coming too! I'm going to get my grandparents out; they'll never manage it on their own."

She was right. Great-Uncle Gerhard was an old man of eighty-seven, and his wife was almost blind. But suddenly I found myself caught up in a reversal of roles, warning and seeking to dissuade Otti, painting the grimmest possible picture of the dangers, the likelihood of disaster, the many opportunities for failure. Aunt Dolly, scared to death, took my side. To no avail: Otti stood there, head held high, prepared to hurl herself into the surf. She was somewhat younger than I, and aglow with eagerness. She was also in excellent physical condition, not just from going back and forth across the border; until the end of the war she had broken in horses for the Wehrmacht. I saw myself beaten with my own weapons: the more I portrayed the journey as arduous and dangerous, the more essential it seemed that we help those who could not help themselves.

"Am I supposed to live the next fifty years with the knowledge that I left my grandparents in the lurch? No more arguing now. We're leaving tomorrow night. And now we're going to get some sleep."

Actually I felt very pleased with the way things had turned out. Having warned Otti, I had appeased my conscience and could now enjoy the prospect of having a companion. Everything seems easier when there are two of you: you can comfort and support and encourage each other. As Schiller's Don Carlos says, "Arm in arm with you . . ." Oh, I had to get over this mania for quoting. It had seen me through the winter, but now spring was here.

Crossing the border into the Russian zone presented no problem. Otti knew all the secret paths to the nearest railway station on the other side. Before sunup we were sitting safe and sound on the train to Berlin. It filled up quickly from stop to stop, until there was an alarming crush; swarms of people laden with whatever food supplies they had managed to round up, all heading for the starving metropolis. The crowding offered protection against identity checks.

Or did it? Of course we all knew—even the authorities—what this antlike rushing back and forth signified. So when the train reached a suburb of Berlin and came to a halt, it was suddenly surrounded by police. "Everybody out!" Cursing, screams, panicky attempts to run, thwarted by the cordon of guards.

We, too, had contraband with us, a little schnapps and—more important by far—one and a half cartons of American cigarettes, the universally accepted hard currency, which we were counting on to smooth our way into the unknown. We had to save them, at all costs.

What should we do? In front of the broad staircase leading to the other platforms and to the municipal railway, policemen holding hands had formed a barricade. What if we suddenly ducked underneath that chain and made a dash for it? Others would doubtless follow us, but we would be the first. The devil always takes the hindmost. No words were needed; a glance at each other, and we scooted under the hands and arms and dashed off. In the surge of people following our example, the police chain broke. We heard furious voices barking orders, whistles calling for reinforcements, pounding feet, confusion. In no time we got clear of the crowd and reached the municipal railroad platform.

Unfortunately, it was not like the movies; no train was standing there on the point of pulling out, so we could not squeeze through the doors as they were closing and thumb our noses at our pursuers. There was just a half-destroyed shelter with a bench in it and two giggling young people sitting on it. We ducked underneath and hid. From above we heard a whisper: "A pack of Ami smokes for a couple of tickets—you'll need them."

Obviously two sharp kids, quick to strike a deal. We made the exchange in a hurry and emerged innocently from beneath the bench—just in time. The transit police appeared, shone their flashlights in every nook and cranny, and demanded to see tickets. Those who had them were in the clear. Those who did not were shooed back down the steps, no matter how they begged and pleaded. The train arrived and carried us into Berlin.

Back to the Malinowskistrasse in Zehlendorf and the ministrations of Ilse Hagens and Gretchen Voigt. We spent the next day on a scouting mission that took us all the way to the Stettin Station, set amid a landscape of ruins. Did the name still signify anything? Had we any chance of getting to Pomerania from there? We heard the same answer over and over again: no, no, no.

Still, while asking around, we ran into a young woman who had something to offer us. She came from East Prussia and had been hauled off to Siberia. There she fell seriously ill and was allowed to go home. She still had her certificate of discharge, a paper with Cyrillic writing and some impressive rubber stamps. Because her East Prussian village had become inaccessible, the paper named no destination but merely said that the woman was released to go "home." She had been taken in by relatives in Berlin, was properly registered as a resident, and had regular identification papers now; she did not need her Russian document anymore. Might it come in handy for us? It certainly could not hurt. So the certificate of release changed hands—at a price, of course: a pack of Lucky Strikes.

If not Stettin, how about Angermünde? Trains were operating from there to Scheune across the demarcation line. And that was where Otti and I set out for, after a second night at Aunt Ilse's. She hugged us affectionately, and

Gretchen touchingly provided us with sandwiches, which we could not refuse, even though we knew they came out of their sparse rations for "average consumers."

In peacetime the train from Berlin to Angermünde had taken barely an hour, with a stop in Eberswalde. Now, however, the train could not get under way, no matter how the signalman exerted himself with his red cap and green flag. The train merely gave a jerk, perhaps a signal of good intentions, or perhaps the aged and infirm locomotive's cry for help. How could it be expected to get up a head of steam on that coal slag, a dismal substitute for real coal? Finally, after three false starts, the train began to creep along, wheezing asthmatically, with long pauses to catch its breath at every station and even in between stations. Fortunately, there were no hills to climb; otherwise the passengers would have had to get out and push. It was night when we arrived. For the second time in the space of a few weeks, I found myself in the dilapidated waiting room in Angermünde, with my sleeping place behind the bar.

"Wake up!" Kicks and shouts. We jumped up in panic. This time no friendly Russian with a crust of bread, but two ferocious figures toting submachine guns. "Move it! Quick! Quick! Under arrest! Interrogation!" They had already picked up two young girls, and the four of us were marched off into the unknown. Or rather, it all too soon became apparent what was in store for us. We were not heading into town, where the Kommandatura and the prison would be, but in the opposite direction, past the freight station, warehouses, and train barns. Where to? Somewhere off in the dark must be a deserted shed or hut. There no one would see or hear what happened.

No lights, no more station, just the tracks. The first guard went on ahead, leading the procession. Then came the two girls, then Otti and me, then the second man. After a while we noticed that he had fallen behind. He stopped, and we heard him talking with someone. Laughter rang out. He must have run into some buddies whom he was urging to come along for the fun. Otti and I fell back too. The soldier in front marched on without looking back; he heard the two girls close behind him. On our right was a fence with a steep embankment behind it. There were gaps in the fence. A squeeze of the hand, a poke in the ribs, and we jumped, rolled down the embankment into the dark—and straight into a thicket of brambles.

They could scratch and prick us all they liked, so long as they gave us cover, while up above all hell broke loose: shouts and running feet. The girls' frightened cries, shots. Flashlights were flicked on. We lay flat on the ground under the bushes, waiting for quiet to return and the voices and footsteps to pass on. We did not move an inch; someone might be lurking up there, waiting.

How long did we lie there among the thorns? I strained my ears—and at the same time my thoughts wandered in a strange direction:

> But no sooner had the spindle pricked her finger than the prophecy was fulfilled, and she fell down lifeless on her bed. However, she was not dead, but had only fallen into a deep sleep; and the king and the queen, who just then came home, and all their court, fell asleep too. And the horses slept in the stables, and the dogs in the yard, the pigeons on the roof and the flies on the walls. Yes, even the fire on the hearth left off blazing, and went to sleep. . . .

But this time it was no hundred years. A few minutes, perhaps, then we cautiously crawled out into the open, first crouching, then running across lots to put distance between us and our persecutors. Finally we stopped, panting for breath. We looped back into town and tried the doors of buildings, hoping to get off the street; there might be patrols about. At last we found an unlocked doorway and spent the rest of the night on a flight of cold stone steps. Only now did we notice that we had scratches all over and thorns caught in our hair, our skin, and our clothes. But mixed with the bother of picking them out was a sense of triumph, almost of gratitude: that bramble thicket had proved our salvation.

JOURNEY TO POMERANIA

But there went a report through all the land, of the beautiful sleeping Rosebud (for so was the king's daughter called); so that from time to time several kings' sons came, and tried to break through the thicket and into the palace. This they could never do; for the thorns and bushes laid hold of them as it were with hands, and there they stuck fast and died miserably.

Sugar and Steamed Potatoes

"For heaven's sake, get out of here, girls; they've spent half the night looking for you!" When we sought out the stationmaster the next morning, he was horrified to see us still around.

"We want to get out—but to Stettin. When will there be a train?"

"To Stettin? Are you out of your minds? Where do you think you are? No, no, there aren't any trains."

Stettin was no more than sixty-three kilometers away, but we might as well have been asking for tickets to the moon.

"How about freight trains, then?"

What a question to ask an employee of the German Railways! He shifted a ruler on his desk, adjusted his glasses, leaned back, and put on his most forbidding official mien. "Now, ladies, first of all, freight trains are for freight and not for passengers. And second, there are no freight trains. Well, there are sometimes . . . but only Russian trains. Is that clear? I suggest you put it out of your minds and get out of here."

Russian trains! How could we get on one? We put our heads together and decided to venture into the lion's den, to the Kommandatura. After all, we did have our certificate of discharge, and perhaps we could brazen it out.

The commandant, when we were allowed in to see him after some back-and-forth, was a friendly man. Volubly and with eloquent gestures, we described our plight: as returnees from Siberia, who wanted to rejoin our families near Stolp in Pomerania but were being prevented from doing so by the

Poles. The innuendo worked like magic: the commandant nodded vigorously and said, "Yes, yes. Poles bad. Very, very bad. But Russians good. Just ask Russians. Russians always help against Poles."

We had uncovered a mixture of age-old and brand-new resentments between these two neighboring peoples, allies and brothers-in-arms though they now claimed to be. The commandant wrote something on our paper, signed it, and stamped it. The fact that the discharge certificate was rather old and was made out for only one person he had either overlooked or disregarded.

"Not forget: Russians good, Russians help."

We left, assuring him with extravagant gestures that we had always assumed this to be the case and would never forget it. Confident that nothing could stop us now, we headed straight back to the station.

And sure enough: there stood a long freight train, guarded by Russian soldiers. We waved our piece of paper at them and asked to see their commanding officer. The officer turned out to be a boy of no more than eighteen or nineteen in a lieutenant's uniform. We produced our discharge paper and told him the sad story of our attempted return home, already so embellished in its second telling that it practically had us in tears. What we heard then filled us with excitement: the train was carrying a load of sugar destined for a ship in Stettin harbor. We asked whether we might hitch a ride. We doled out cigarettes. Why not? The lieutenant laughed, his men laughed, they pointed out a brakeman's cabin. "There—there. Good to ride in!"

And so it was, or at least it might have been. These old-fashioned structures, stuck onto the cars like large nesting boxes, seemed almost cozy; next to the brake lever there was even a board you could pull down to sit on.

In the meantime, the laughing, chattering soldiers were milling around us, probably not only on account of the cigarettes, whose popularity was reducing our precious stock rather alarmingly. The soldiers seemed to want to see how many people could fit into the little cabin. The longer this continued, the more uncomfortable the situation became. Behind all the laughter and chatter we sensed a threat. So we fought our way outside and sat down by the tracks at some distance.

At long last the locomotive steamed up, pushing another car ahead of it. The eight German railwaymen who composed the train's crew could hardly have been more amazed to see us if we had been little green men from Mars. "I don't believe it. Girls, girls, be sensible, stay home! What do you think you're letting yourselves in for? No one ever tried this. It'll turn out badly–it's sure to. They'll make mincemeat of you!"

And so on: they painted the disasters in store for us in the most lurid colors. But apart from that, they had no objection. If the Russians agreed to our going along, why not? Besides, we would provide a bit of variety in their monotonous routine, and our cigarettes were nothing to sneeze at, either. Last but not least, a kind of roguish ambition came over them: perhaps they could put one over on the Poles.

"All right, girls, if you're determined to hurl yourselves into disaster, we don't want to stand in your way."

The car that the locomotive had pushed into place held eight bunk beds for the railwaymen; they offered it to us as a place to spend the night. Of course we accepted gratefully. Why not take advantage of a bunk? Some of the men would have to be on duty, in any case. "As comfortable as a sleeping car, I'll guarantee you."

Actually our trip to Pomerania could begin now. The locomotive had built up plenty of steam–too much, even: it had to let some of it off now and then. Since it was pulling freight for the Russians, it got real coal, not that dusty slack. But our departure kept being delayed. The signals stubbornly stayed red.

"You see how it is, girls?" one of the men said in irritation. "I suppose there's some kind of dispute again. The Poles aren't happy to see the Russians carrying off this booty, so they're probably saying that a switch is stuck, or a bridge is blocked, or something. Or the ship it's supposed to be loaded onto hasn't come in yet. I wish they'd all go to hell."

"And in the meantime we're starving," another added. "They don't care if our stomachs turn inside out. All this sugar, it's no treat for *us*."

But there was something we could do to help. We had noticed a mountain of potatoes a slight distance away, guarded by a Russian sentry. Otti and I strolled over to him. Otti employed her conversational skills and a Lucky, while I quickly and stealthily filled my rucksack with potatoes and made myself scarce. Otti followed when the sentry had finished his cigarette.

Now we had really won the hearts of the railwaymen: "Girls, you're tops!"

"But they're raw," we said.

"That's easy to fix." They put the potatoes in a sieve and held it under a steam valve in the locomotive. The extra-hot steam both cooked and cleaned them in no time. "Look at that: A-one steamed potatoes, courtesy of the German Railways." They had a can of salt in their sleeping car, and we enjoyed a splendid meal. There was even some left over for the next day.

After two hours or so, the signals finally changed to green; the locomotive whistled, and we were off. We did not get far, however. The train kept having to stop, and every siding seemed to have been put there to test our patience.

When darkness fell and the train was stopped again, the Russians demanded that we join them in their car: "Woman drink vodka. Vodka very good." We declined as politely and firmly as possible and tried to make ourselves scarce. But it was not that easy. One man pursued us with particular insistence. We fled to the locomotive and, a few seconds later, dashed along the other side of the train, while the driver sounded the whistle to signal that departure was imminent and shunted the train back and forth. Otti, a little ahead of me, jumped in through a half-open door. She tried to pull me in behind her. But the Russian had caught up with me and grabbed me by the legs. A tug-of-war ensued between heaven and hell, or rather, between the load of sugar inside and the embankment outside. Struggling, I gave a good kick behind me. The Russian fell back, cursing. Then the train stopped shunting and finally moved off.

I was struggling to catch my breath and regain my composure. We might be safe for the moment, but we knew we were balancing on the razor's edge. If we really angered the Russians, they could simply throw us off the train, or turn us over to the Poles on arrival. Certainly the idyll of the sleeping car was out of the question; we spent the rest of the night finding a new spot at every stop, as swiftly and unobtrusively as possible.

The following morning, though we were still far from Stettin, everything seemed innocuous again. The lieutenant and his men enjoyed the breakfast cigarettes we handed out. One of them asked. "You sleep good, woman?" Good-natured laughter all around. The man who laughed the loudest was my pursuer of the previous night, who was taking his misfortune like a sport: "Woman boot very good." Unpredictable creatures!

It took us half a day, an entire night, and the better part of the next day to cover those sixty-odd kilometers to Stettin. In the last few hours of the trip, behind the demarcation line, our Russians proved their worth. Each time the train stopped, they swarmed out, submachine guns at the ready, as though they, too, were in enemy territory. They allowed no one to approach the train. From the secure vantage point of the moving train, I pointed out to Otti the sugar factory in Scheune, and the damaged tank that had sheltered me.

Lady Luck

So now we were safely in Stettin, or more precisely in Stettin harbor. We could see at a distance the burned remains of the venerable castle of the dukes of Pomerania, and the Prussian administration building up on the Hakenterrasse. That was where my great-grandfather once lived and held office, the one who had left us the emperor's old watch. After his stint as a minister, he was Governor of Pomerania from 1891 to 1899. Mother had visited him often when she was a little girl, and she would sometimes tell us about the impressive old man with his handsome white beard.

Now entirely different gentlemen occupied the seat of power, and it did not seem advisable to visit them. In any case, we had a problem to solve first. The part of the harbor we were in was strictly cordoned off; it was the free port, which the Russians had reserved for themselves. The railwaymen, for instance, were not allowed to leave this area and had to stay in their sleeping car until the train departed. All the access roads and pontoon bridges had Polish customs officials and militia posted, who would immediately arrest any stowaways—particularly if they were German.

So what could we do? Our friends had nothing to suggest. They shook their heads: "We told you it would turn out badly." But because they had taken us to their hearts, they offered us one solution: "Be sensible. We'll hide you and get you back home." Home? Where was that? We did not want to go back to Angermünde again; we wanted to go on to Stolp.

In our hour of need, a guardian angel appeared. The Russian lieutenant came to say goodbye; he had to report to his headquarters in town. And he immediately understood what was causing us such distress. "No trouble! I arrest women, then go to Kommandatura." He fetched his submachine gun, pointed it at us, and put on a menacing air, grinning all the while: "Move! Quick! Quick!" So we trotted along ahead of him, obediently hanging our heads and looking woebegone. As we passed the Polish sentries, they just cursed obscenely and offered our escort sniggering advice. We were two German women getting what we deserved. The lieutenant cursed back cockily and hustled us along even faster. When we had passed all the checkpoints and said goodbye at a street corner, we both felt like hugging this big boy in the dreaded earth-brown uniform. But circumstances forbade that; passersby were beginning to eye us inquisitively.

The bombing and the arrival of the Russians had almost completely destroyed Stettin's old city; we saw Saint Jacob's in ruins. But already new life was stirring; many people were hurrying busily back and forth. In one bombed-out area, they formed into little clusters: it was the center of the black market. We had no time, however, for melancholy reflections. Evening was fast approaching, and we had to solve our next problem: getting off the street and finding a place to stay. Nowhere in the Polish zone were Germans allowed out after dark. If we ran into a patrol, since we had no papers and no evidence of a job or a place to live we would be arrested and clapped in prison.

How would we find lodgings? The best thing was probably to ask other Germans; they had to be living somewhere. You could recognize them easily by their shabby clothing and their timid, skulking manner. They seemed to take up less room in the street than the victors.

We decided to ask a woman almost hidden under her large gray shawl, who came scurrying around the corner toward us. As we hurriedly explained what we needed, she looked us up and down with understandable suspicion. But when she learned that we had just been smuggled in from the West, and when Otti flashed a pack of Lucky Strikes as proof, her attitude changed in an instant. Again, very understandable: people here had no reliable information on conditions "over there," only rumors, and no one would want to miss an opportunity to get news firsthand. If we could have traveled around freely, giving our information to whoever wanted it, we would have been carried in triumph through the land and into people's houses, as now in fact happened.

"What a coincidence! Yes, I do have room, a big building not far from here. . . ." She gave a Polish street name. "It's a bit damaged, but it's being fixed up, by German prisoners of war. The Russians want to move their Kommandatura in there. At the moment it's empty. I just guard it; I'm the cleaning woman and concierge there. Come back in an hour, and I'll be waiting for you. I just have an errand to run first."

No sooner had she hurried off than we ourselves were addressed. A middle-aged man whom we found difficult to place asked us if we could tell him where to spend the night. We were the suspicious ones this time: where was he from, where was he going, and why? The man explained that he was a Czech from Bohemia. He had been swept into the German army—and his fiancée was waiting for him in Hamburg. Then, with a small bow, he introduced himself: "Heinrich, Count Kinsky."

"Really? The family of the General Kinsky in Wallenstein's army?"

A second bow. "Colonel, madam, not general. Just colonel. Murdered three hundred and twelve years ago with my commander in Eger, on February twenty-fifth."

"I must say, you seem pretty alive to me," Otti exclaimed, and was rewarded with a third bow.

"And what on earth are you doing now? Here, in this devastated Stettin?"

"In such times one tries to get by. You are acquainted with our national hero, the good soldier Schwejk? The Poles, of all people, have just given me a job as a long-distance truckdriver."

"A long-distance truckdriver? In what direction?"

"Unfortunately, the west is barred—for the present. So it's east. Tomorrow morning I'm driving to Danzig."

That made us prick up our ears. Even though this count seemed rather gypsy-like to us and might or might not be the real thing, it would be folly to ignore such a sign from fate. A lift in return for a place to stay?

A fourth bow. "By all means. Word of honor. And I guarantee you a safe hiding place in the back when we get to the roadblocks where they check papers."

Another sign from fate, as good an omen as one could imagine: our landlady turned out to be called Frau Glück—

Lady Luck. Of course, she was not overjoyed when we introduced her to her third guest. But her curiosity won out, and what she had to offer us was overwhelming: a large building with long corridors and many empty rooms. We chose a basement room that boasted two advantages: a washbasin with real running water, and a rear exit. If a Russian patrol or the Polish militia came stomping into the building, we could slip out quietly and hide in the surrounding ruins.

But first we met the German prisoners of war who were working there. They were as astonished to see us as the railway men in Angermünde. "It's incredible you managed to get into Stettin, girls! And now you want to go east, across the Oder, to Stolp? Oh boy, oh boy—that won't be easy."

And then it was like Christmas. Before they had to return to their barracks for the night, the men brought us all sorts of things from the attic, storerooms, and cellar: an old sofa, a table and chair, a stove complete with pipe, which they pushed out through the window opening, and wood for heating. "Good night, then. See you tomorrow!"

Frau Glück gave us a thorough grilling. What was life like under the British or the Americans? Was there plenty of everything? It was like a fairy tale there, wasn't it? Sampling a Lucky Strike, she closed her eyes and said in awed tones, "Ah, yes, there's high civilization for you." But soon we had to beg off for the evening. In the delightful warmth of the stove we could hardly keep our eyes open. After all, we had just spent two sleepless nights in Angermünde and on the train to Stettin. We consigned the count to the sofa, while we lay down on the floor under a blanket of Frau Glück's. We slept very soundly; our emergency exit would probably have been useless, because no amount of slamming doors, clattering boots, or rattling weapons could have waked us. But thank God we were left undisturbed.

One ID Too Many; or, Magic Wand and Soothsayer

We slept far into the morning. When we finally woke up, the POWs were sawing and hammering again upstairs. For breakfast, we had some of our bread form Berlin and hot water.

Our count had also overslept. Wasn't he supposed to have reported to work early? But no, he showed no signs of haste. "You must realize, ladies, that the Poles are no Russians, thanks be to their Holy Virgin. Besides, the truck has to be loaded first. There's plenty of time for me to get there."

Perhaps. But sensing our skepticism, our good soldier Schwejk produced his ID—or rather, two IDs, one Russian, the other Polish. The name was Kilki, not Kinsky. Of course, that might be one of the subterfuges called for by these times, in which proletarians, not aristocrats, were in favor. Then he even produced a third document, in English this time. God knew—or the devil, more likely—what all this signified, and what perversion of legitimacy they represented. They served to confirm rather than allay our suspicions. "One ID too many," Otti said dryly.

Thereupon the man pulled out his trump card, which was literally up his sleeve: a magician's wand. "Ladies, look at this. An old family heirloom, handed down from father to son. Very valuable, and at the moment virtually my sole possession."

Truly a strange item: a slender wand of darkened rosewood, about twelve inches long, inlaid with tortoiseshell and ornamented with three silver rings. In the middle and at both ends was gleaming carved ivory: at one end something like a crown, with two polished bones attached that rattled, and at the other end a hand with an extended index finger, presumably for swearing an oath. "As I say, this is a very ancient family piece."

"Dating back to Wallenstein, perhaps?"

The familiar bow. "I would neither deny nor affirm it. Its

origins are lost in time. In any case, this wand has been lost or stolen many times over the years, but it has always returned to its rightful owner. The finder, and even more so the thief, falls into such an abyss of fear that all he can do is return the wand as quickly as possible."

"And what can one rightfully do with it?"

"Hypnotize people, for example. But please understand: silence and secrecy are necessary for it to be effective, as they are to the family honor. But I wanted to say: I'm going now, and I shall leave my heirloom with you as a pledge."

"For goodness' sake . . ."

"A pledge. The wand and its owner are never parted for long. Till later . . . I'll be back in two or three hours with the truck."

And with a final bow he went out. We waited nervously for two, then three hours. We waited out the afternoon, and the evening. Herr Kilki or Count Kinsky never returned.

"I knew it—I smelled a rat right away. The man's not to be trusted," Frau Glück said sagely. "I felt a chill run down my spine the minute I set eyes on him. The evil one. Didn't he have a little limp?"

If he did, we had not noticed. "One ID too many," Otti said again. "probably they frisked him and found it. Perhaps they identified him as a former Wehrmacht soldier. Or worse, as an agent, a spy, SS, Gestapo. Something like that. And then it was good night, Heinrich."

I know, this story sounds so bizarre, so farfetched, that no self-respecting novelist would touch it. But it is true, and I can prove it: today, forty years later, I still have that wand. Incidentally, it never caused me any apprehension, let alone fear.

But back to March 30, 1946. As we sat in our basement quarters in Stettin, we tossed around theories as to where the master magician might have come from and where he had gone. Perhaps he would turn up after all. Perhaps the truck was not loaded, or it had engine trouble and had to be repaired. But what should we do if he failed to come? There was little we could do in any case, other than sit and wait.

Frau Glück had a deck of cards, which we borrowed to pass the time. We played patience, or sixty-six. The prisoners kept popping in, and sometimes one of them stayed for a quick game of skat. Finally, late in the evening, by the light of a candle also contributed by Frau Glück, I started telling Otti's fortune. I did it with elaborate hocus-pocus, chiefly for the benefit of our landlady, who was looking on spellbound. I even got out the magic wand, which she had not seen yet, and waved it over the cards. In the spooky light, the ivory finger pointed to kings and queens, knaves and aces.

Of course, the results I achieved were spectacular: "I see a journey, Otti. No, not this one, but one to come. A great journey, across a great body of water. And now . . . wait, what's this? This conjunction of the queen of hearts and the knave of hearts! Otti, I see a man come into your life. He's handsome, his eyes glow like coals, and he has dark, curly hair. And he's wealthy too . . ."

And so on. Frau Glück was speechless with amazement. She was so excited she was almost afraid to breathe. "Is it possible? I wonder if . . . could you . . . for me too?"

Why not? The good woman had already spread her entire life before us, confided all her hopes and desires. I found it easy to astonish her by coming up with things from her past and then leading her that much more confidently into the blooming garden of a still hidden but near future. She went off to bed happy, almost reverent: "Good night. I'll never forget this evening."

"Good night, dear Frau Glück."

This nocturnal scene, never meant to be more than something to pass the time, bore unexpected results. The next morning, apparently at the crack of dawn, Frau Glück hurried around to tell all her friends and acquaintances about the wonderful fortune-teller with the magic wand. No sooner had we chewed our breakfast bread—which, for all our abstemiousness, was almost gone—than she appeared to ask whether, as a great favor to her, we couldn't tell her friends' fortunes. And from that point on, there was no letup. Our playfully tossed snowball had started an avalanche. The friends and acquaintances told their friends and acquaintances, and the stream of visitors continued uninterrupted.

One could understand why. We human beings know about the future, but not what it will bring. And we have to live with that uncertainty. Faith helps us, or skepticism. Or superstition; the more uncertain the times, the more threatening the circumstances, and the less we are capable of determining the course of our own lives and guessing more or less what the next day will bring, the greater our need to entrust ourselves to the stars, the flight of birds, the roll of the dice, the tea leaves, or cards. And the greater also our readiness to be led or misled if someone turns up who, while he cannot really see into the future, has such insight into our hopes and fears that he can read the dark depths of our hearts.

But there was the rub. We knew Frau Glück but not all those who followed in her wake. So we had to organize the sessions. Otti received the visitors in an anteroom and chatted with them while they waited; she explained that the clairvoyante was busy with someone else or needed time to meditate and attune herself to the next visitor. The ambience was also important: we hung our blanket over the window and lit the candle, and I wore a kerchief pulled down over my forehead and shading my eyes.

When Otti came in to find out whether I was ready, she would quickly whisper to me whatever she had managed to discover. Getting the information was not difficult; the visitors came in full of their cares, only too eager to unburden themselves. But I had to concentrate very hard to read their expressions and find exactly the right blend of concrete detail and suggestively vague allusion. By evening I was completely done in.

Otti managed to guide our services into the proper commercial channels. Of course, she did not charge any fees as such. But she did give people to understand that they should dig deep into their pockets to support the great fortune-teller, who was far too immersed in her clairvoyancy to be able to think of such earthly necessities as food. Soon we had what we needed: enough food to put an end to our problems and to promote Frau Glück to the role of cook. We received money besides; business was blooming, and our kitty was filling up with zlotys.

Daughter, the Victory Chicken

"That's all for today," I said, exhausted, on the evening of my fourth day as soothsayer.

"No, no," Otti whispered to me. "One more. Pull yourself together, make one last effort. There's someone out there from the Polish postal service. Railway postal service, in fact; a medium- or even high-ranking official. If anyone can get us onto the train to Stolp, he can."

Poles who spoke some German, most of them women, had started appearing among our clientele by the second day. However deep the gulf between the two peoples at present, acquaintanceships quickly came about in the course of daily contact. Shared experiences and growing familiarity built bridges across the divide. Over such bridges wandered word of the fortune-teller. Among the Poles as among the Germans, I met many people who were seeking lost loved ones. The war and its aftermath had ripped families apart; husbands and brothers, parents and children, had dropped out of sight. Were they still alive, would they ever be found? I heard grim stories of violence suffered. What sad fates! Tears flowed copiously. The Germans were not the initial victims of this catastrophe; they had unleashed it themselves. I often found it difficult to maintain my pose and not simply say, I'm so sorry, I have no idea where your Wladislaw is, but I very much hope you find him.

So I pulled myself together and made one last effort. A staid older man came in. He was looking for his two sons and a daughter. Another life full of the wounds and scars of our glorious century. The man came from Posen, had been a German soldier in the First World War, and had fought in the Second as well, only this time as a member of the Polish resistance. His children had been dragged away to the "Reich" as forced laborers. Once more I was assailed by scruples about playing this role. But after I had brought the session to a conclusion satisfying to him, we started again, with reversed rolls: Could he help us get to Słupsk, to Stolp?

"Trains are running. The next one leaves tomorrow at ten. It's not difficult to get you on it. And then . . . then you just need some—luck. Do you have money for tickets?" We counted out our accumulated take. "That's enough: give it to me. I'll buy the tickets, and tomorrow morning I'll come here and pick you up."

Of course, we were taking a risk. The man might disappear without a trace, like our Bohemian count. But what could we do except jump onto this spinning wheel of fortune and hope it stopped where we wanted it to. Frau Glück, though, was inconsolable. Things had never been this exciting; she had never felt as important as she had in this position of mediator to the outside world. Besides, a share of the food that had streamed into the house had gone to her. She prepared a real feast for us on our last evening.

In the morning, everything ran smoothly. The postal or rail-postal official appeared; he handed us our tickets and, with a smile, two Polish newspapers—"as camouflage, an old partisan trick." He escorted us to the station, through the checkpoints, past the militia swarming all over the platform, to where the train was already waiting, with its sign, so welcome to our eyes: "Szczecin—Słupsk—Gdansk." Then, with a nod to us, he disappeared.

We found a compartment whose only other occupant was an honest-looking woman, perhaps a farmer. We slipped into the corner seats and opened our newspapers. The windows were boarded up, but through the cracks we could glimpse the dreaded police uniforms moving back and forth. Gradually the train filled, including our compartment. I was feeling more and more tense. In the dim light, the words and letters swam before my eyes like will-o'-the-wisps.

Finally the conductor shouted, "All aboard!" and the engine's whistle tooted. We were moving, or rather creeping along. Crowds of heavily armed men at the railway bridge over the Oder. Not police, but troops in battle dress. Steel helmets and machine guns behind sandbag fortifications. Were there saboteurs, werewolves, partisans from the German or Polish underground planning attacks? We had no way of knowing. Once on the secure East Pomeranian side, the train picked up speed.

Stargard, and a long stop, far too long. On the platform, civilians were outnumbered by men in uniform. When we finally got moving again, the conductor looked into the compartment to check our tickets. No problem. But then, just when we felt relaxed enough to wink at each other, we heard the thud of heavy boots. The militia coming through to check identification papers.

Instantly Otti and I were sound asleep, the newspapers over our faces. The whole compartment must have heard our hearts beating. The back of my neck felt ice-cold. Memories flashed by. If this had been a German train, during the war, with the Germans in control, they would have shown us no mercy. Whether quasi civilians in long leather trench coats or Wehrmacht patrols in steel helmets, they would have ruthlessly shaken us awake. But now the Poles were in charge, not the Germans, and they respected the sleep of the just.

After a while we "woke up" and looked at each other. I had the impression that Otti's face had not merely gone pale; it had taken on a greenish tinge. "You should have seen yourself!" she told me later. Without thinking, we broke open our last pack of Luckies and inhaled the smoke deeply.

Maybe that was a mistake; all our fellow passengers stared at us and sniffed the unfamiliar aroma. The man next to me said something to me. Was it a match he wanted? I handed him one, and a cigarette to go with it. That seemed to work. To avoid the pitfalls of conversation, we spent the next few hours either sleeping demonstratively or reading the newspaper, burying ourselves in articles of which we comprehended not a word. Why did the train have to take so long? Why these everlasting stops? In peacetime the train had covered the stretch in three and a half hours; now it took that long for less than half the distance. Eight, nine, ten hours passed. The day was almost at an end.

At last we approached Stolp. The train stopped just outside the station—the signals were red. Could they be delaying us until they posted militia to catch the outlaws, travelers without passports, just as they reached their destination? Not necessarily; there were any number of perfectly good reasons why we might have to stop. Probably our imaginations, stimulated by previous terrors, were playing tricks on us. But why take the chance? We looked at each other, jumped to our feet, grabbed our rucksacks, and headed for the door. Suddenly a voice said, in German, "Try the other side, Fräulein!"

We froze and turned around. They were all looking at us, laughing heartily. They said in chorus, *"Auf Wiedersehen!"*

So the newspaper trick had not fooled them; our fellow passengers knew perfectly well what we were.

How simple it would have been to turn us in! A nod to the waiting militia at any one of the innumerable stops would have been sufficient. But no one had betrayed us. If it's a matter of depriving the hunters of their booty, of tricking the authorities, even their own, the Poles enjoy it.

"Thank you, thank you so much, *auf Wiedersehen! Do widzenia!*" We jumped free of the train.

It was dusk, and not difficult to circle the railroad yard and vanish undetected. After all those hours of sitting, it felt good to be walking again. I stormed off in the lead, while Otti vainly warned me, "Slow down, be careful; you have to take your time when you're stalking."

Nonsense; I had gone this way dozens of times, and I knew all the danger points and all the places to take cover. It was twelve kilometers to Karzin. Just before midnight we tapped on the window at Grandmother's and Hannah Brandt's. Astonishment, an emotional welcome, a brief report. Then to bed on the hard "Russian cot." It felt like a luxurious four-poster.

In the morning we walked the last twenty kilometers. It was the kind of April day you dream about. Gentle sunshine, spring in the air. We heard robins, blackbirds, even larks trilling already. We passed the familiar villages: Lankwitz and Sorchow, Silkow-Schwerinshöhe and Gutzmerow. The station at Bandsechow, long since without tracks. Then our forest, the Wossek. The first houses of Rumbske.

Our arrival, our passage through the village, created a sensation. Cries of "She's back! Libussa's back!" preceded us. The women peeling potatoes at the distillery dropped their knives and rushed out, Marie in the lead. Everyone wanted to hug me, and Otti too, or at least shake our hands; everyone wanted to ask questions. What was it like in Germany, in the Reich? "Later, later, please. There's plenty of time to tell you all about it!" We could hardly make our way through the crowd.

Mother, long since alerted, was waiting quietly on the bench in front of the cottage, with her granddaughter, my little girl, on her lap. She hugged me with deep emotion, but she quickly regained her self-control. "Not a moment too soon, child," she said, and "Happy birthday!" I had completely forgotten: it was April 5, the deadline I had set for my return.

No sooner were we indoors, and Marie had put the water on for coffee, than we heard a knock at the door. There stood the Polish mayor, laughing, with a sack in his hand: "Daughter good, chicken good. Bet lost, too bad. Daughter beat Poland. Very, very good." He handed me the sack and elegantly kissed my hand. "Daughter, the victory chicken."

And that became the bird's name: "Daughter, the victory chicken." In the happy expectation that she would lay eggs, we gave her a place in the attic at night, as protection against weasels and other thieving creatures. In the daytime she was tethered behind the house and allowed to grub for worms. But it soon became apparent that her fertile days were long past. Daughter, the victory chicken—the oldest and toughest fowl the mayor had been able to find—went into the pot. To us she tasted just fine.

Epilogue

From Pomerania to Holstein

Since returning from the West, I had been plagued by a strange ambivalence, a feeling of being out of place. I could hardly account for it. Rumbske was my home, where I had been born and raised. I knew every twist and turn in the road, every tree, all the people. I still encountered smells I had known since childhood. I knew the inside of people's houses. And for almost a year now, in spite of everything, I had felt quite at home in the gardener's cottage.

Yet now that I knew that Holstein could offer my child the security that no longer existed here, all I could think of was leaving. One cannot feel at home in a place where one has no sense of safety. In such circumstances, all that remains is the bitter path of exile, and the exile's wistful memories of what once was.

My thoughts of leaving were clouded by my own terrifying experiences, of which I had given Mother only a very mild version, so as not to alarm her. I kept having flashbacks of the attacks on the train, the nightmare in Scheune. What could we do? I discussed it with Otti, and we decided first of all that we should wait for midsummer. The shorter the nights, the better for us, because darkness favored the attackers.

Somewhat later we learned of a new development: territorial Polish administrative offices were being set up. And in Zipkow, one of the villages in the parish of Glowitz, a director had already been installed. He was said to be approachable. Could he help, perhaps by providing a useful document? We went to find out.

Yes, the director did exist. He had taken up residence in the manor house as its new lord, and he received us in lordly fashion, kissing our hands like a Polish cavalier. A slim, well-groomed man of about fifty, he spoke excellent German: "Please be seated, ladies. What can I do for you?"

Before we could begin, my eye was caught by his desk. An astonishingly familiar sight: it had once stood in my mother's room in Rumbske, an elegant Empire escritoire. So not everything had gone up in flames.

The director understood my reaction without my saying anything. A gesture, a smile. "Yes, this desk. I found it here when I arrived. It's beautiful, don't you think? And it's full of memories, almost like an heirloom for me too. . . . That's the kind of furniture we used to have, before the Germans came."

Otti pointed to an ancestor portrait on the wall: "Herr Direktor, that's a Puttkamer from Glowitz."

That smile again. "I know. That's why I have it here; there are Puttkamers among my own forefathers."

What an encounter! For a moment the walls of insanity that our modern age had thrown up between the nations vanished. The director regretted all the more that he could not help us; emigration to the West lay outside his area of responsibility. But he provided us with a useful contact: "A good friend of mine and a senior railway administrator in Słupsk—pardon me, in Stolp."

So we walked to Karzin, and from Karzin to Stolp, where we looked up the administrator. What he told us sounded promising. The exodus had recently been reorganized. Somewhere in the upper echelons, where destinies were shaped, there had obviously been some dissension, not to say a blow-up. At least we could infer as much from the allusions we heard. The British had apparently protested about the condition in which people were arriving from the East. For a time the transports had been halted altogether. Now the resettlement was handled train by train, via a newly established camp near Stettin. "Not Scheune anymore, but Neu Torney." If one reported to the militia in charge and registered properly for emigration, everything would take an orderly course.

"Without any attacks on the train?"

"Yes; guaranteed."

It sounded almost too good to be true. We had no choice, however, but to hope for the best. Next we had to make our way to the militia in Glowitz, where I had been put in the stocks to be spat at barely a year before. This time we got registered for emigration without any difficulty; we did not even have to pay. We were simply informed that it might take a few weeks; the lists were long. "You'll be notified three days ahead of time."

In the meantime, we made our arrangements. Mother's mink was sold to the mayor's wife in Glowitz. We got a very poor deal, but what else could we do? We would have had little chance of getting it safely to the West, and we desperately needed zlotys to buy flour and proper yeast for bread, and some pots of lard. A small sum of money might come in handy on the trip too, for bribes or necessary purchases.

Next we set about adapting the perambulator. We installed a false bottom, where our savings passbooks went, and all the money we still had from the estate safe—about 8,400 reichsmarks. We unscrewed the hollow handle of the carriage and slipped Mother's pearls inside.

Finally we made a kind of last testament, stipulating how our belongings would be distributed among Grete Krupps, Fräulein Rahn, and Grandma Kreft. By peacetime standards we might not have had much, but things like beds, chairs, a frying pan, and a saucepan were worth their weight in gold now. Marie had a difficult decision to make: to whom could she entrust her valuable heirloom? In the end, it went to Frau Vietzke, in gratitude for her saving little Claudia's life.

Then came the painful farewells in Rowen and Rumbske. Tears flowed. Would we ever see each other again? No one said so, but everyone realized that it was highly unlikely, especially in the case of the older people. When Mother returned from seeing the old Vietzkes and the Hesselbarths, she did not speak for a long time afterward; a word might have cost her her self-possession. Marie, though, said what she felt: "It's too much to bear."

But we had to bear it. We sat there with our bags packed, or, more precisely, one suitcase and three rucksacks. Together with the baby carriage, which was to carry bed linens and towels, that was all we needed for our sparse belongings. But nothing happened. Days and weeks passed, and already July had come. At last a woman arrived from Glowitz with news that Otti, Great-Uncle Gerhard, and Great-Aunt Lena had been scheduled for departure. But Glowitz was one thing, the surrounding villages another. They had different lists, and we could not travel together. We could not go with our relatives in Karzin, either.

Then, finally, a militiaman came with our marching orders: we had to be in Neu-Klenzin by noon the next day, not a moment later. When we arrived, however, they put us in the former inn there, and two days passed, during which no one paid the slightest attention to us, still less to feeding us. Fortunately, we had zlotys, with which I went shopping in nearby Glowitz. Others lodged with us had to depend on their own scarce provisions for the journey. Not until the third day did a tractor pulling a trailer arrive to take us to Stolp. Another night, this time in a large, empty hall in an extensive complex of buildings that was filling up with émigrés. On the morning of the fourth day, we proceeded in a long, baggage-laden column to the station.

This time the train did not have sections for the conquerors and the conquered, merely cattle cars for the Germans. Much time was spent calling the roll and assigning people to cars. It was afternoon before we departed. This train, like all the others I had traveled in recently, seemed to be trying to win a prize for slowness. It took two days and two nights to cover a stretch of 237 kilometers—an average of five kilometers an hour.

At least the doors remained unlocked, and we were allowed to get out at the stations. We first headed for the rest rooms, then looked for water, because the heat in the windowless cars was oppressive. Often our search proved vain; the water mains were dry because the pumping stations were not working. We also had to stay very alert, because we never knew whether the train would leave in an hour or the next minute. Once, I came across the mobile water crane that supplied the locomotives. Without much hope, I tugged at the chain, unleashing a waterfall all over myself. I stood there like a soaking-wet poodle, while the others laughed. But the cold shower felt wonderful.

The train's jerky starts and stops caused a half-tragic, half-comical problem in our car. One of our fellow passengers was a paralyzed man in a wheelchair, who could not operate the brake himself. Every time we speeded up or slowed down, the chair would go shooting across the floor, a "one-man torpedo," as Mother said, not exactly life-threatening but still a dangerous situation for the man and the other passengers. Someone had the obvious idea of blocking his wheels with luggage. But somehow the wheels kept working free, especially when everyone was dozing and not on the lookout. Suddenly the torpedo would go lurching, and we could not always catch up with him before he crashed into a wall.

Also among the passengers was a strangely silent young couple with a child. It took me a while to realize what their silence meant: they were Poles, not Germans, smuggling themselves out among the pariahs to escape their own new masters. I found that a little hard to grasp, until I recalled the ride with Otti in the forbidden train from Stettin to Stolp; I knew how terrified they must feel. So at every opportunity I nodded and smiled encouragingly at the couple. Eventually they understood what I was trying to express, and they smiled back shyly.

Two days and two nights for the first stage of the journey, and all the time I was haunted by the fear of being attacked. But in this essential respect the Stolp railway official's promises turned out to be accurate: we were indeed spared.

The transit camp at Neu Torney was a barbed-wire-enclosed compound containing a few houses and barracks. It was hopelessly overcrowded. The idea of having connecting trains for the next leg of the journey was obviously not working out, and new arrivals would have to sleep under the stars. I went looking for Otti, who had left only a few days ahead of us. Maybe she would have organized some better quarters. Sure enough, Otti was still there. Somehow she had acquired a Red Cross armband and, with its help, had secured a room for her grandparents. They took us in, just in time to save us from a violent summer storm with high winds, hail, and torrential downpours.

Otti's claim to a room was not entirely unjustified. Great-Uncle Gerhard was at the end of his strength and mentally confused: his body had set out on the journey, while his spirit remained behind in Glowitz. Otti felt terrible and was blaming herself for wanting to uproot an old tree; maybe she should have waited, so he could be laid to rest in his native soil. I tried to reassure her: "You did everything in your power, and you meant well."

Certainly, but what comfort was that when the old man kept calling for his horse and cart so he could ride out into the fields to check on the rye crop?

There were holes in the camp fence, and supervision was lax. During the very first night I slipped out to have a look at the surrounding area. I came across a cemetery, torn up by bombs or shells: toppled crosses, bones and skulls, lay everywhere. The following night, by moonlight, I went back to the cemetery and buried a leather pouch containing the money and jewels that had been in the perambulator; maybe we could get them past Polish customs this way. But the night after that, I shamefacedly dug up my treasure again. By this time I had observed that departing Germans were escorted from the camp gates directly to the railway station—under close guard. To reassemble the baby carriage without tools proved difficult and cost me several fingernails.

In the course of my exploration I discovered street vendors hanging around the perimeter of the camp; they were selling things we needed, at moderately or immoderately inflated prices: bread and butter, milk and fruit. In this instance our foresight in selling Mother's mink for zlotys paid off: we could purchase things to replenish our own dwindling supplies, while others in the camp were feeling hungry. The daily meal provided for the emigrants consisted only of watery soup and a very small amount of bread.

After two and a half weeks, Great-Uncle Gerhard, Great-Aunt Lena, and Otti were cleared for departure. I helped carry their luggage to the borderline, which I was not allowed to cross, not yet. As we said goodbye, the old Glowitzer looked at me for a long time. His mind cleared; he recognized me and said, "My sister Elisabeth is your grandmother, isn't that so? Give her my regards and tell her I'll be coming to see her shortly." He was referring to the "Iron Countess," who had died a few years before.

We spent three weeks in Neu Torney, a suburb of Stettin, until finally our day, too, arrived. Beyond the camp gates, in a barbed-wire alley, tables had been set up for the baggage inspection. Mother and Marie got through, but I aroused suspicion. "Every carriage—hidden valuables," growled the experienced customs official. "Baby out!" But the baby had not only filled her pants; she had also, as a result of the irregular diet of the last few weeks, been suffering from diarrhea and had soiled the sheets and towels under her. The smell was truly awful. Disgusted, the customs official turned away. "German pig—move on!" That was fine with us.

There stood the train, our train. And this time it had real carriages, meant for human beings. It even had new glass in the windows. "Welcome!" was chalked on several of the doors, and the compartments were decorated with greenery.

What a transformation! We were going to Lübeck. There we got out for a "British welcome," as someone told us over a megaphone. Rows of tables and benches had been set up under trees. "Take a seat!" we were told. Volunteers appeared, carrying steaming bowls. The adults got a hearty meat broth, the children sweetened porridge and hot milk. For dessert the children received something they had certainly never seen before, a banana. One boy stubbornly resisted—clearly he was a true Pomeranian, following the old principle: "What the farmer don't know, he don't eat."

While we were eating, a British officer went from table to table. "Are you all right?" he asked. "Are you getting enough to eat? Help yourselves, there's plenty." I saw many people burst out crying, and some of them wanted to kiss the hand of this unfamiliar type of victor. He tried to hold them back. From the next table, the young Polish couple waved to me happily, all their anxieties gone.

"All aboard, please. The train is leaving for the reception camp."

All aboard—but why? Where were we going? Right here we were very close to our destination. The German official who was apparently in charge said something about a place near Hanover.

"But that's the wrong direction for us; we want to get to Holstein."

"Impossible; out of the question. Schleswig-Holstein is closed to immigration."

"But here is my immigration permit."

Apparently he had not yet encountered anyone already equipped with a permit, and for a few moments the fellow floundered. But he quickly recovered, and phrases like "orderly process" and "regional quotas" rained down on me. It all sounded so strange and confusing, and there was no time; the train was already blowing its whistle for departure. So I let myself be bowled over; we climbed aboard and set off in the wrong direction.

The reception camp served only as a transit camp, where we were provisionally registered. Soon we heard that we would be moving on to a "final" camp—once again in the wrong direction, far to the west in Wipperfürth. But by this time I had pulled myself together, and I had had enough. The camp had no barbed wire and no sentries; they were counting on German obedience, not reckoning with people like us. We simply walked out of the camp and set out on our own. Apart from the overcrowded trains, we encountered no difficulties. On August 8, 1946, we reached our new refuge.

A few weeks later, I heard from Otti that Great-Uncle Gerhard had died that day in Wipperfürth.

Breaking Down Fences in Leipzig

We lived in two small rooms and had the basic necessities. It was all on a very modest scale, of course. Our table, our chairs, and our beds came from discarded furniture found in various attics. We cooked on an old-fashioned, not very reliable cooker out in the hall. But we were not fussy. The coming winter held no terrors for us; we had an iron stove and a good supply of beech logs from the nearby forest. How to split and stack wood properly we had learned long ago. The Reventlows—in the First World War the count was in Father Jesko's regiment—lived nearby, and the countess helped us out with potatoes, dried beans, and oat grits, even though her own large house was filled to bursting with refugees. For Marie I found a job with some friends in Hamburg who were still well off.

But the more we settled into our newly won security, the more we worried about Father Jesko. Since his being moved from Stolp to Danzig, we had had no word of him whatsoever. And how about news of us? How would he find out we had resettled in the West? In Schleswig there was an agency that specialized in translating letters into Polish and sending them off. Whether they ever reached their destination, no one knew.

Petitions to the authorities took up a lot of our time. We needed coupons for a dress, a coat, and a pair of shoes, because we had next to nothing left to wear. A song of Erich Kästner's that was going around described our situation perfectly:

In the last thirty weeks or so,
I've moved around an awful lot.
My shirt has sprung so many leaks, y'know,
It's like a sieve that's gone to pot.

My shoes have uppers but no soles,
My rucksack is my trunk.
My furniture is with the Poles,
My cash in the Dresden Bank.

I've got no home and no relations,
My boots could use a shine.
Is this a cause for celebrations?
The Decline of the West is mine!

The authorities refused to budge: "Either a dress or a coat, not both!"

"For two adults and a child? And how about shoes?"

"Not possible. Put it out of your head."

So I went back to my eighteen-month habit of stalking. Perhaps something would turn up. But I did not go on foot now; I took the train, horribly overcrowded though it always was. Or hitched a ride with truckdrivers, who had to stop every few miles to fiddle with their wood-gas generators.

Since I had no wares of my own to offer, the effort of traveling over greater or lesser distances became itself my stock-in-trade. It worked like this: Someone in Hamburg gave me a silver candlestick to take to a friend in Cuxhaven, who would give me some canned fish to deliver. I could keep a couple of cans as my commission. These I took to Kassel in the American zone, where I could get a good price for the nutritious fish. By adding a little cash of my own, I could buy a whole carton of cigarettes, which were relatively inexpensive there. In the Russian zone these American cigarettes were particularly rare and sought after, and in Chemnitz I could get the nylon stockings that a master shoemaker in rural Holstein wanted for his marriageable daughter's dowry. In exchange for the nylons he made me a splendid pair of stout shoes that I desperately needed. And so on: I brought a seaman's duffel bag from Berlin to the West; I ventured all the way to Marktheidenfeld near Würzburg, where Frau Liebe and Hannah Brandt had been taken in by my mother's sister, Aunt Annemarie. Only the onset of winter forced me to suspend my operations.

This winter of 1946–1947 brought the coldest temperatures in years. We hardly ventured out of doors, because our only coat, bought with the coupons, was far too thin for such cold. We thought all the more about Father. What could things be like in Danzig? "Don't be sad. Much better there. Heat in winter," the prison commandant had assured me when Father was transferred. But I had never quite believed him.

The weeks passed, then months. Even this terrible winter eventually passed; spring came, early summer. One morning I was awakened by a knock on the door—a telegram: "Baron Puttkamer in Russian camp Leipzig. Müller."

The name Müller meant nothing to me; presumably a fellow prisoner of Father's had been released. But the telegram galvanized me; surely it was a cry for help. I promptly decided to go to Leipzig. Would I be able to accomplish anything there? Would I even get to see Father? I had no assurances of anything, but I had to try.

Friends with whom I stayed in Hamburg gave me something really valuable: the address of someone in Leipzig, a Fräulein Küchenmeister, formerly governess in Sommerswalde Castle. I made the trip without incident; by now I knew the secret paths over the border into the Russian zone.

When I arrived, I found myself in a sea of ruins. But the house I had been told to go to remained intact. At first Fräulein Küchenmeister seemed unfriendly and frightened. What if I ran afoul of the Russians and they found her address on me? I assured her that I had never written down her name and address but had committed them to memory. But what really changed her mind were the two tins from a CARE package, sent along by the friends in Hamburg. I spent the night on the floor of the tiny place that the governess shared with her sister.

Apparently everyone in Leipzig knew the Russian camp. I had no difficulty finding it, for everyone I asked pointed me toward the suburb where it was situated. Barracks surrounded by a fence, facing on the street. I strolled by, looking as innocent as possible. Barbed wire and Russian sentries patrolling—not much one could do here. But how about the rear?

Railway tracks and an embankment, and then the fence, back here made of vertical boards with barbed wire strung along the top. No sentries, at least not on the outside of the fence. I climbed the embankment and peeped through a crack between two boards. A prisoner came into my field of vision, only a few yards off.

"Psst, can you hear me? Don't look this way! Stand with your back to the fence, please, so no one will notice."

The man did as I instructed him. I asked, "Do you know Baron Puttkamer? Jesko von Puttkamer—is he in the camp?"

The man's reaction was astonishing: "Libussa! You must be his daughter Libussa!"

"How do you know?"

"He always said, 'My daughter Libussa will come.' We've often teased him about it."

"Can you bring him here?"

"It's a bit difficult now. He's off working. But in the evening, when it gets dark . . ."

"All right. Tell him I'll be here, at exactly the same place."

I looked at the fence again. The planks were nailed at top and bottom to horizontal members. It should not be too difficult to loosen the nails at the bottom, swing the planks aside to create an opening, and then swing them back into their original position. All I needed was a pry bar.

I went back to town, where I bought two tickets at the railway station. My hostess was horrified when I asked her for a pry bar. She denied having anything of the sort.

"But you must have some tools."

"Well, in my storage cubicle in the basement . . ."

I found a proper toolbox there—complete with pry bar. Poor Fräulein Küchenmeister—the anxiety I subjected her to! Admittedly, my own heart was pounding that evening as I slunk along to the agreed-upon rendezvous, the burglar's tool up my sleeve. But almost everything went as planned. Father Jesko was already standing there, with his back to the fence. "Father!" I called softly.

"Libussa!"

I quickly explained my scheme: We would meet here before dawn, and he would slip out through the gap. Then we would go to the station and back to the West. . . .

The last thing I would have expected was objections. "No, Libussa, I can't do it."

"For heaven's sake, why not?"

"Because I'd be putting you in danger. It won't work out, it can't possibly work out. Mother needs you, your baby needs you, and in prison—"

"Nonsense. It'll work out, of course it will. I've gone this far now, and I want to see it through."

It was no use. Father's qualms were like huge boulders across the path, and I could not budge them. Our whispered argument lasted longer than it should have; we were going around in circles. Then I changed my tune: "Father, please help me. Otherwise I just don't know what to do. I've no money left, nowhere to stay, nothing, only these two train tickets. Please, Father, what's to become of me?"

That did the trick. Unexpectedly forced into the role of protector and possible savior, Father had no choice but to cooperate.

"One thing, though, Libussa: some of the others will want to come too."

"Oh, no, for goodness' sake! They'll discover the break-out immediately, there'll be a general alert, and the station will be cordoned off. Then we'll be in real trouble."

"But—"

"No; you're not to tell any of the others!"

"They're my comrades."

"Then tell them to behave accordingly. We need a twenty-four-hour head start. They can do whatever they like, so long as they do it the day after tomorrow."

And that settled it. Father went off, and I applied the pry bar; the planks loosened easily, and I could push them to one side and back. Early in the morning, Father crept through the opening, we headed for the station, got on a train, and were off. The only further difficulty was hiking across the border by night.

When dawn lit up the sky, I saw a small hill ahead of us. I said, "Come on, let's climb up there."

"No, no, they'll see us."

"Never mind; come on."

Once at the top, we sat down in the grass. I had one cigarette left, half for each of us. I pointed to the rising sun. "Look, Father, that's the East. And there's the border. We're over it."

"My God, Libussa, can it be true?"

Yes, it was true.

A Homecoming and a Farewell

Father Jesko was terribly thin. The tall, broad-shouldered man now weighed just a little over a hundred pounds. So first we had to try to build up his strength. That was not so easy. As a welcome-home present, our landlady, mistress of the estate, gave him exactly one egg; it remained her only contribution. The rations for "average consumers" had hit rock bottom during this hot, dry summer. And for the time being, Father did not even qualify for rations, because he could not produce an immigration permit or a certificate of release. He was still a nonperson in the eyes of the law. It took me weeks and finally a whopping bribe to change that.

At least Countess Reventlow helped in any way she could, but even her resources were stretched to the limit. So I took to the road again, procuring whatever I could on the black market. Clothing needed to be "organized" as well. My moaning about the situation induced friends to offer a few items, but real help came only when an unexpected parcel arrived from donors in Sweden.

The aftereffect of Father's imprisonment was profound exhaustion. He slept very late, and in the daytime he wandered off to the deserted Baltic seashore nearby, where he buried himself in the sand and rested. Besides this, he was completely passive, so much so that Mother sighed, "He won't even open a door for himself." But it was understandable: for two long, bitter years, others had unlocked doors for him and bolted them again behind him.

Only gradually did a change occur. But it was coming; it had begun almost imperceptibly. And then we were invited one day to dinner at the Reventlows'. Father Jesko looked surprisingly elegant. He had put on a dozen pounds or so, and he was gradually growing into his Swedish suit. The hours of sunshine on the beach had done their part to dispel his pallor. An excellent dinner was served: venison with whortleberry sauce. Candles gleamed, wine flowed, afterward we had coffee, and the gentlemen helped themselves to cigars. Old times seemed to have returned—and Father Jesko with them. He talked animatedly, delighting the ladies with his charm and the count with his memories.

"Ah, yes, August 1914—our advance through Belgium . . . Remember our colonel, Reventlow? He was quite deaf. When the shells began crashing about our ears, I called to him, 'Grenades, Colonel!' 'Pardon? Close shaves?' 'No, grenades!' 'Really?' And a few seconds later . . ."

Baptism by fire! The air was so pulsing, so overflowing with maleness, that one would have liked to weep, without knowing why. . . . Then rapture draws maleness so far out of itself that the boiling blood drums against the veins and seethes through the heart, an intoxication beyond intoxication, release, shattering all bonds. Madness unbounded, like only unto the forces of nature. Man is like a torrential storm, a turbulent sea, the roaring thunder. Then he merges into the universe. Like a bullet toward its mark he hurtles toward the dark gates of Death. And when the waves close purple over his head, he has long since lost awareness of the transition. It is as if a surge were gliding back into the flooding tide.[17]

The old boys, reminiscing about the adventures of their youth, the everlasting replay, all this "remember when" talk—it infuriated me. But as we walked home under a starry sky, I felt almost happy. Father Jesko had come through, he had woken up, he was finding his way back to himself.

Our happiness was short-lived. In fact, it collapsed no sooner than it had appeared. Father Jesko did indeed find his way back to himself: back to the baron and officer, to Prussia and Pomerania. He had stationery made with a letterhead that said "Puttkamer-Rumbske." The unpleasant present hardly counted, unless as a waiting room, an exile of limited duration. At some point everything that had once been would be gloriously restored.

Doomed worlds; ghostly, haunted castles: at least that was how it all looked to me. Was the past innocent; had it no connection with Germany's descent into disaster? Even if this past had been blameless, what could it contribute now but rigidity and unhappiness, because in its mirror the present was bound to be a bitter disappointment. Did not new circumstances call for a fresh approach? Recollection, in wistfulness and even love, was one thing, but facing the future was another altogether. In short, tension inevitably arose between Father and me. And our quarrels became frequent.

There was another, decisive factor. For Father, part of returning meant reestablishing the ancient division of labor: the man of the house vis-à-vis the womenfolk; the protector vis-à-vis the protected; the provident father vis-à-vis the dutiful daughter. Unfortunately, I could no longer play this role. Circumstances had changed all that.

Father Jesko looked for work and a source of income. He gallantly accepted whatever came along. He worked in road construction and felled trees, and he worked hard. And why not? To be sure, it did not bring in much, apart from respect and self-respect: an hour's wage would not even buy a cigarette. But that did not stem the flow of his injunctions: I should give up these travels of mine, this vagabonding about, this dealing on the black market. "You're staying home now; you have your baby to take care of."

"Nonsense. Mother takes care of her perfectly when I'm away."

"But the black market and all this profiteering aren't proper."

"Excuse me, Father: what do you think is keeping us alive? Your piffling wages, maybe?"

We worked ourselves into a hopeless rage. Father banged on the table: "So honesty has gone to the devil, and with it honor. I suppose you'll take up stealing next?"

"We already did steal, if you remember. And if I had to, I'd do it again, with Mother—no matter what you said!"

"Libussa!"

"No, listen to me: for whose sake do you think I started all my traveling and vagabonding about anyway?"

Father went red in the face. He drew a deep breath and roared, "Don't think I have to be eternally grateful to you, just because you saved my life!"

"I wouldn't dream of it!" I shouted back. "You have my word. And I wouldn't do it again!" With that I ran out of the room, slamming the door so hard that the whole house shook.

Of course neither of us meant what we said in our fury. It was not a question of gratitude or of doing it again. It was a question of who and what we were. The things I had learned in the dark years now behind me, the confidence and independence I had developed—God knows, they were bought at a price, and I had no intention of giving them up, whatever the cost.

My mind was made up: tomorrow I would be on the road again. I would go to Kiel, where the British were based. I spoke good English. A job as a secretary, an interpreter, a housekeeper, a nanny: something would turn up.

EPILOGUE

Afterword to the English-Language Edition

This book ends in 1947, but the story did not.

Libussa did indeed find work with the Occupation Forces, first as a housekeeper for an English general, then as a secretary for the French. At some point she learned that her husband, Jobst von Oldershausen, had been killed in the last weeks of the war. Later she married a doctor and in 1953 emigrated with him to Mexico, where they lived for the next thirty years.

Claudia, the child born under such dramatic circumstances in March 1945, the child for whose survival Libussa fought with such tenacity and wily resourcefulness, grew up in Mexico and there met her husband, an American from Ohio. Today they live with their children in Florida.

These transformations in the personal realm mirror drastically altered political and social circumstances. As an ancient elite, the Prussian aristocracy had kept to itself and regularly intermarried; Libussa's first marriage still adhered to this pattern. But her son from her second marriage has a Japanese wife and lives in Washington. I have a Chinese daughter-in-law, and grandchildren who are half-Chinese.

Of course, my family cannot be called typical; most Germans still marry Germans. Yet one could not call my family completely atypical, either. More and more, Germany has opened itself to the world; the inhabitants of Central Europe have become world-champion travelers, and it pains them to recall that once upon a time they sang, in arrogant isolationism, "Deutschland, Deutschland, über alles . . ."

When Dr. Fritz-Osner retired from the practice of medicine in 1983 and he and Libussa returned to Germany, a house happened to be for sale next door to me in Göttingen. So the returnees became my neighbors, and only this proximity made it possible for me to write this book. For it was more than a matter of my simply taking notes while my sister talked. This project of remembering, which conjured up long-repressed terrors, involved a difficult and painful process, almost like undergoing psychoanalysis. Libussa had never before told this story. Her daughter learned of it for the first time from the finished book.

Apparently Libussa needed to put several decades' distance between herself and these events before she could venture into the past. Even then her mind seemed to resist bringing to the surface matters so fraught with pain. Only gradually, in the course of many long conversations, did she begin to open up—but then the memories gushed forth. More and more often my sister would resume our talks with the remark, "Last night it came back to me . . ." It was a liberating process, and she felt a great weight had been lifted from her soul.

Can this same process be applied to entire peoples as well as to individuals? After 1945 the Germans had no desire to remember things the majority of them had applauded and the things they themselves had done. They concentrated instead on hard work and achievement. "The D-mark and gold medals constitute the core of the German national identity," a historian has remarked critically of the postwar period. The fact that their country found itself divided, with each part soon on opposite sides in Cold War alignments, furthered the process of repression. Only gradually, in the face of much resistance, has a transformation set in—especially since 1968, when a new generation began to interrogate its fathers mercilessly, with the innocent self-righteousness typical of the young.

The German-Polish relationship made for a particularly troublesome chapter. The Holocaust, with its murder of millions of Jews, was too horrifying, too enormous to be ignored. But much less was said about what the Poles had suffered under German rule, and would have continued to suffer, had the Germans won. To make things worse, the Germans now protested that they had been bitterly wronged: in 1945 Germany lost, under pressure from Stalin, almost a third of its territory, land in the East that was turned over to Poland. And millions of people had to flee their homes under the inhumane conditions described in this book. In the West, influential organizations of expellees soon sprang up. They inveighed against the injustice perpetrated on them, generally speaking as though the whole thing had begun only in 1945, and demanded the return of the lost territories.

In Poland a similar phenomenon occurred, although in reverse. Official parlance recognized only "liberated" and "regained" territories; allegedly the area in question was "ancient Polish territory." In truth it had never belonged to Poland, at least not within the era when the modern nations and nation states took shape, and Germans had lived there unmolested for centuries.

How can we escape from this vicious circle? I am convinced that the first requirement is to renounce retribution and seek reconciliation. For that reason the borders created in 1945 must not be tampered with; to do so would unleash violence again, with no end in sight. Besides, with the passage of time it becomes increasingly clear that borders turn rigid and impermeable if one batters against them, whereas they can turn into bridges if one calmly accepts them. My own home may lie in the lost German lands in the East; but for my grandchildren, born in the West, the picture looks different—as it does for the Polish children growing up where I spent my childhood; they are the third generation. And if we really love our children and our grandchildren, we must do everything in our power to save them from the horrors we once experienced.

Since her return from Mexico my sister has emphatically supported me in this position. Together we traveled to our old home and sought contact with the people living there. Over the years a real closeness developed; these strangers have become trusted acquaintances, even friends. Among Germans our behavior has occasioned ambivalent reactions. Eventually the majority came to support and respect our stance, all the more so because we hailed originally from the East and as an "old family" had had large holdings there. A minority, however, took recourse to invective, often demonstrating its courage by delivering its message anonymously: "You traitors, go back to your Poles, since they pay you!"

The most recent developments have dramatically altered all political relationships. As the price for unity, and to avoid filling its neighbors with fears old and new, Germany has been forced to recognize, solemnly and once and for all, the established borders, especially the one with Poland. Does that settle the matter? We would like to think so, but we do not really believe it. Political events can come precipitously and give rise to unexpected situations, for which people's hearts are not yet ready. The hearts must find their own way, slowly and painfully.

Will they find it? In May 1990 something happened that moved my sister and me deeply: *The Hour of the Women* appeared in its first translation—in Polish. The book was brought out in the very place where forty-five years earlier the victors in this story had avenged themselves: in our town of Stolp. So this book, which contains many episodes that must be extremely bitter for Poland, was understood—not as a call for further vengeance but as liberation from it, through the power of memory. This response allows us to hope: for our children and grandchildren, for reconciliation and peace.

CHRISTIAN, COUNT KROCKOW

Notes

1. The first lines of the Wehrmacht report for June 15, 1944, in *Die Wehrmachtsberichte 1939–1945,* Vol. 3 (Munich, 1985), p. 127.

2. Wehrmacht report for October 7, 1944, op. cit., pp. 278–79.

3. Wehrmacht report for December 18, 1944, op. cit., pp. 370–71. This report goes on to give an account of the defensive fighting in Italy and in Hungary. The nature of the war at home is characterized in the concluding passage:

> By day, American bombers on terror missions have been attacking targets in Upper Silesia and the southeast of Germany. At night, the British made another terroristic raid on the center of Munich, once again violating Swiss neutrality. Considerable damage was done to residential quarters, and to historic and other public buildings, among them hospitals. Bombs have also fallen on Ulm. Rhineland-Westphalia has been another target. Our air defenses have downed 36 Anglo-American planes, including 24 four-engine bombers.

4. Wehrmacht report for January 13, 1945, op. cit., pp. 399–400.

5. Wehrmacht report for March 2, 1945, op. cit., pp. 467–68. The report for the following day proclaims: "In bitter fighting in the east of Pomerania, our troops have prevented the enemy from extending their breach of our defenses." In actual fact, it was that same day that Soviet advance detachments reached the Baltic coast in the area of the Jamund and Buckow lakes, thus finally cutting off East Pomerania.

6. Letter from a German officer stationed in eastern Poland, dated October 31, 1939, in Hans-Adolf Jacobsen, *Der zweite Weltkrieg:*

Grundzüge der Politik und Strategie in Dokumenten (Frankfurt/Main, 1965), p. 43.

7. From the report on "results in the USSR," no. 10, by the chief of the Security Police and the Security Service, October 7, 1941, in Jacobsen, op. cit., pp. 184–85.

8. Wladyslaw Bartozewski, *Herbst der Hoffnungen* (Freiburg, Basel, Vienna, 1983), p. 86.

9. The second section of the final Wehrmacht report for May 9, 1945, op. cit., pp. 569–70.

10. Hans Frank, governor-general of occupied Poland, on March 26, 1941, quoted in *Das Diensttagebuch des deutschen Generalgouverneurs in Polen 1939–1945,* ed. Werner Präg and Wolfgang Jacobmeyer, Publications of the Institut für Zeitgeschichte, vol. 20 (Stuttgart, 1975), pp. 338–39.

11. "Special order" on "The Preservation of Military Discipline," issued on September 10, 1941, by the commander in chief of the Fourth Army, Field Marshal von Kluge, quoted in Helmut Krausnick and Hans-Heinrich Wilhelm, *Die Truppe des Weltanschauungskrieges—die Einsatzgruppen der Sicherheitspolizei und das SD 1938–1942* (Stuttgart, 1981), p. 230. The order was issued with instructions that it subsequently be destroyed.

12. Bartozewski, op. cit., p. 115.

13. Governor-General Hans Frank, official diary entry for May 30, 1940, op. cit., p. 212.

14. Heinrich Heine, "The Lorelei," trans. Aaron Kramer, quoted in *Bartlett's Familiar Quotations,* 15th ed. (Boston, Toronto, London, 1980), p. 481.

15. From a speech by SS Reichsführer Heinrich Himmler to SS leaders in Posen, October 4, 1943. See "The Trial of the High War Criminals Before an International Tribunal, Transcripts and Documents," Nuremberg, 1947–1949, volume XXIX, p. 122f. and 145. Quoted by, among others, J. C. Fest, *Das Gesicht des Dritten Reiches—Profile einer totalitären Herrschaft* (Munich, 1963).

16. Erich Kästner, "Die grosse Suche nach dem Alibi," in *Kästner für Erwachsene,* ed. Rudolf Walter Leonhardt (Frankfurt/Main, 1966, pp. 466 ff.

17. Ernst Jünger, *Der Kampf als inneres Erlebnis* (Berlin, 1922), pp. 12, 53.